# THE WORLD OF
# AMISH QUILTS

# THE WORLD OF
# AMISH QUILTS

## Rachel and Kenneth Pellman

Good Books®
Intercourse, Pennsylvania 17534

# Acknowledgments

Design by Craig Heisey

We wish to give special recognition and thanks to Rebecca Haarer who helped collect quilts for photographing and served as a consultant for this project. We are also pleased with the way Jonathan Charles captured these wonderful masterpieces on film. In conversation with local Amish neighbors we found both quilts and valuable information. For that we thank those friends. Merle Good granted special permission to reprint "Song of a People," © 1969. We are grateful to The People's Place for permitting us to borrow "Excerpts from a Grandmother's Dairy" for this project. And finally we were warmed by the cooperation of the many folks who generously permitted us to exhibit their treasured quilts on the following pages.

# Photograph Credits

Cover photos: Jonathan Charles

All photos throughout the book were taken by Jonathan Charles except the following:

Jerry Irwin, 1, 25 (top), 82; Kenneth Pellman, 8, 11, 20 (bottom), 24, 32 (bottom), 40 (bottom), 45, 46 (bottom), 62 (left), 63 (top), 68 (bottom), 80 (bottom), 88 (bottom), 100 (bottom), 104, 105, 126; David Lauver, 9, 25 (bottom), 44, 58 (bottom), 92 (bottom); Richard Reinhold, 12 (bottom), 26 (bottom), 100 (bottom), 62 (right), 63 (middle, bottom), 64 (bottom), 72 (bottom), 84 (bottom), 106 (bottom), 110 (bottom), 114 (bottom); Steve Scott, 76 (bottom).

**THE WORLD OF AMISH QUILTS**
Copyright © 1984 by Good Books, Intercourse, PA 17534
International Standard Book Number: 0-934672-22-9
Library of Congress Catalog Card Number: 84-080651

# Table of Contents

*Prologue*

# The World of Amish Quilts

How can the splash of color, synonymous with many Amish quilts, well up from a people whose life is so reserved and disciplined? Is it not both a visual and theological irony for the "quiet-in-the-land" to mix such austerity and beauty?

An encounter with antique Amish quilts is incomplete if it does not include some understanding of the people who made them. If one studies Amish quilts without relating the finished textile to the community of its origin, one is left with only a partial look at these wonderful bedcovers.

The Amish are traditionally recognized for their strict lifestyle. Black hats, drab carriages and sad faces are quick labels often used to identify them. But by wearing the right kind of glasses—those that look beyond oversimplification—one will discover that the Amish live in a delightful world of faith, community and beauty.

Beauty and craftsmanship are traditions among the Amish. Meticulously manicured lawns and gardens, correctly shocked stalks of field corn, well groomed houses and barns belong to their way of life. They find joy in the push of a bean through the springtime soil, in filled chairs around the supper table, and Sunday visits. Loaded canning shelves and full hay mows satisfy their bodies and spirits. To do something well and attractively is always more gratifying for them than doing one of those qualities without the other.

## Who Are These People?

Who are these people? Where did they come from? Where are they going? Why do they live the way they do?

The Amish are, most basically, a people committed to God. They believe that their lifestyle and practice must embody their faith. They intend to live, in every part of life, consistently with Jesus' teachings in the New Testament.

The Amish believe that Jesus taught his followers to be a community to each other that nurtures its members to

greater faithfulness. It is from this unique belief that the Amish receive much of the solidarity they need to continue living with the tensions they feel with the outside world. One cannot be Amish alone. It requires the support and fellowship of others who share the same beliefs. The community becomes the conscience for the individual. And the community discerns together the do's and don'ts for its members.

## Community is a Refuge

Most Amish do not see their community as restrictive. Rather, it is a harbor from rampant Western individualism they believe responsible for the demise of the church, home and family. It is against this backdrop that the Amish church continues to grow, having doubled in size in the last twenty years. There is peace, security and joy in living as the Amish do. Though not without its struggles and problems, the Amish community nurtures its members in wonderful and precious ways.

So as a result of trying to follow their faith daily in life the Amish find themselves to be separate from the world. And because they are committed to their faith-life, they are wary of anything that could become a possible route to acculturation into the "world." The Amish believe that becoming involved in the larger society takes one away from family, community and church. Their leaders are constantly concerned with the purity of their fellowship. So they tend to draw lines in black and white areas before the issues become gray to help identify their church's separation from the world.

The Old Order Amish (the strictest of all the Amish groups) have traditionally shunned the use of electricity from local power companies, have not permitted telephones in their homes, have rejected ownership of automobiles and usually discontinue their formal education on the completion of grade eight. Their farming is generally

done with horses and mules. Dress regulations are quite severe. Solid colored fabrics are usually the rule for men's and women's clothing. Their primary language within the community is Pennsylvania Dutch (Deutsch) although they are also fluent in English. Yet the Amish are not simply figures cut from the very same form. They are individuals, and as a result, diverse within the structures. It is this blend of diversity and regulation that keeps the Amish culture alive and vital.

# The Problem with Technology

For the Amish, advanced technology is not evil or wicked in itself. They do not think that a vehicle with four wheels that travels at high rates of speed is necessarily designed by ungodly forces. But the Amish do believe that the automobile is a major factor in breaking up the family. A car in the driveway increases the temptation to be places other than home, thus making it difficult to spend the majority of evenings each week with one's family.

The same concern is behind the Amish rejection of electricity from local power companies. The Amish are not opposed to the correct alignment of electrons and neutrons that produces electricity. Their caution is that if it is too readily available in the house, members could be tempted to acquire all kinds of appliances and gadgets that may lead to the accumulation of possessions and luxury. They may buy a radio. And if a radio, why not a television? And if one has a television, why not watch movies that are aired?

And if one watches movies at home, why not go to the theatre and cinema as well? They believe the drift into the world can be subtle. That explains why the Amish are so leery of keeping up with style and technology. Separation from the world, they believe, is a biblical value that also holds them together as a people of god.

While these generalizations are true for most of the Amish groups spread throughout many states, there are always exceptions. Blanket statements can result in an unfair depiction of a people who have individual characters and personalities. So how did these people begin? Where are their religious moorings?

# Not a Fly-by-Night Group

The Amish find their roots in the Protestant Reformation. They are a Christian group whose origins are with the reformers who believed that the break Martin Luther and Ulrich Zwingli were making from the state church was neither as extensive or severe as it should be. At that time in the 1500s, the word "Amish" was not used.

The leaders of this radical left wing of the Protestant Reformation believed in a separation of church and state. One could live peaceably within the boundaries of the state but only with the keen understanding that one's first allegiance was to God. If the requests of the state ever conflicted with the group's understanding of Christ and his teachings, the state would have to take a back seat.

*There is a serenity about the Amish way. Early morning always brings lots of chores to be done around the farm regardless of the season.*

This small group also practiced adult baptism. They believed baptism to be a symbol of one's commitment to Jesus and the way of life he demonstrated while living on earth. Biblical study showed these reformers that the way of Jesus and the way of the world had difficulty coexisting. Because of potential physical and emotional persecution from people outside their convictions, this group believed one must thoroughly understand these possible hazards before committing oneself to following the values Jesus taught. They believed only adult minds had the capability of making such a tough decision. That is why they performed voluntary baptism for adults. Because of this practice, they were nicknamed by their taunters, "Anabaptists." This title does not mean anti-baptist, but rather re-baptized.

The Anabaptist movement officially began in Zurich, Switzerland on January 21, 1525 when the first group of adults took turns baptizing each other. The beliefs of this group found ready acceptance from many people throughout Europe. The movement flourished, spreading quickly through Germany, France, and the Netherlands. A prolific writer and articulate man from Friesland became known as a prominent leader of the Anabaptists. His name was Menno Simons. It's from his name that people in his church were eventually nicknamed Mennonites.

# Church Concerned with Purity

In 1693, a Mennonite minister, Jacob Amman, had a conviction that the church was getting too lax in the enforcement of the discipline that separated them from worldliness. Amman led a difficult and painful split from the Mennonites. The people who followed him were nicknamed Amish.

Because of identical origins and similar faith understandings, the Amish and Mennonites remain much more alike theologically than different. They are like religious cousins. Their differences are primarily evident in their lifestyles and practices rather than in their basic beliefs.

# What Distinguishes Antique Amish Quilts?

The quilts in this book are antique Amish quilts. The dates of their origins range from the mid-19th century to the early 20th century. Amish women do continue making quilts today. But these recent quilts look drastically different from the old ones as a result of modern materials and dyes. These contemporary quilts, though made by Amish, are not included in this collection.

Why have many of these antique quilts gained the attention of art critics in the larger world? Why are they in such demand by collectors? Why are they escalating in value as investment objects? There are many answers. It is nearly impossible to acquire the same fabrics and dyes used in antique Amish quilts. Natural fibers dyed at home with

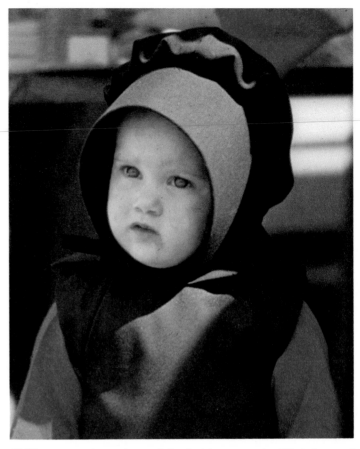

*Children are an integral part of the Amish community. Their dress and language reflect who they are expected to become.*

natural pigments produced a warm vibrance, unattainable in modern fabrics. There is also an exceptional artistic quality present in these quilts.

Art, for itself, is frowned on within the Amish community. Amish women never formally study color or line in an attempt to design an aesthetically pleasing quilt. That a quilt functions warmly and well as a bedcover was a quiltmaker's primary concern. Because these quilts were not designed to be art objects, they become most interesting if they are not removed from the context in which they were constructed.

# An "Innocent" Creativity

Something about the wholeness of life in the Amish community has produced and permitted the mix of superior craftsmanship and visual quality. Creativity has thrived in Amish quilts. The Amish communities' uneducated approach to color has resulted in daring bursts and subtle blends of color. Within the Amish setting little attention is given to color coordinating clothing or home decor. One wears the colors allowed by the church and plants the flowers created by God. It seems to be this freedom from color theory and an uninhibited use of bright colors that has produced some wonderful masterpieces. Not all old Amish quilts, however, fall into this delightful category!

*Turgid colors and geometric shapes are typical in the quilts of this disciplined people. Stars created from diamond-shaped pieces of fabric are common among Eastern and Midwestern Amish.*

# What Inspired These Patterns?

Trying to decide the origin of any given quilt pattern soon becomes mere speculation. But an understanding of the rural agrarian environment that produced these quilt-makers is helpful. Fences around pastures certainly create straight line imagery, depicted in Bars and Rail Fence patterns. Star quilt patterns and the heavenly bodies seem to have a common motif. Fan quilts and buggy wheels may be related. Windmills that pump water and Pinwheel patterns have a similar design. And the parallels between nature and quilt patterns continue. This type of conjecture is difficult to prove. But finding skyscraper, subway or computer motifs in Amish quilts is even more difficult!

Many Amish quilt patterns have specific names but abstract geometric shapes. Realism in pieced quilt tops is not generally permitted by the Amish church. Images are suggested but not definitely constructed. For example, one can see an interlocking log motif in the Log Cabin even though there is no door, roof, or windows. And because of the difficulty of attaching two curved pieces of fabric to each other without puckers, most pieced quilt shapes have straight edges. Squares, rectangles, diamonds and triangles make up the basic group of geometric designs used. The majority of Amish quilts are assembled using these four main shapes.

# Putting Quilts Together

Quilt tops are constructed in two primary ways—by piecing and by appliqueing. Piecing means that the top layer of fabrics on a quilt are sewn to each other along common edges. The result is a single layer of fabric with seam allowances on the reverse side. This piecing is usually done with a sewing machine.

Appliquéing is the process of sewing by hand, one piece of fabric to the surface of another, making sure raw edges are hidden. Because a quiltmaker does not want a quilt to have a puckered surface when it is finished, this procedure is more tedious and time-consuming than piecing. Appliqueing is usually done when curved pieces of fabric are required in the pattern under construction. The tiny hidden stitches of skillful appliquéing are achieved only by long-time veteran quilters.

While straight-edged geometric shapes usually make up the pieced top, the lavish quilting that nearly smothers them is often full of curves and circles. Realism is more acceptable in this intricate stitching. Fruit and flower designs are found occasionally in quilting, alongside the more common feather, plant, waffle, and medallion motifs.

# Quilting Stitches Are Functional

The elaborate stitchery that envelops these bedcovers is

viewed as functional within the Amish world. A quilt is composed of three layers. And the quilting is needed to hold those three layers together. The top is the pieced or appliquéd surface. This side of the quilt boasts the colors and pattern which gives the quilt its name. Quilts also have backs. This surface rarely has any pieced or appliquéd pattern and is the bottom layer of the quilt. (Frequently the skill of the quilting stitches is more visible on this reversed side because there is no variation of color or pieces to compete with the viewer's attention.) Sandwiched between the top and back is the lining. This middle layer provides warmth, but also serves to enhance the quilting. Because the lining is usually thicker than the top or back, its puffy quality shows off the masterful stitches of Amish quilters.

The word "quilting" is both a noun and a verb. The verb "quilting" is the actual process of hand-stitching the three layers of the quilt together. Great care and attention is given to keeping those small running stitches as tiny and straight as possible. With old fabrics and old linings, a good quilter could line up as many as five stitches on a needle at one time and get two full needles' worth of stitches per inch. The finished stitches are also referred to as "quilting." They anchor the lining between the top and back to keep it from bunching up.

## Knotting Comforters

Another method of attaching the layers of a quilt together is by knotting. This process is much less tedious and time-consuming. One stitch with a heavy thread is drawn through all three layers of the quilt and then the two ends of the thread are knotted together on the top. This procedure is done in regular two or three inch intervals. The ends of the thread, which are often a contrasting color, are not clipped closely. Instead the tails are nearly an inch long to be sure the knot does not open. These knotted bedcovers are usually called comforters.

## Diversity in Amish Quilts

People often perceive the Amish to be backward and against all change. But is a group who contributes almost nothing to air pollution, for example, really backward? Their home-grown meat and vegetables lack chemical preservatives; crime and divorce are nearly unheard of within their community. But this is not to imply that the Amish are static. They do experience change, but at a less frantic pace than most of their non-Amish neighbors. Their increased use of diesel power, extensive use of pneumatic tools and appliances, and their more frequent riding of bicycles signal change in some of the communities.

Nor has the quilting world of the Amish been exempt from change either. Pattern types and variations, the size of pieces, and color have all evolved. There are marked geo-

graphical and chronological differences visible in Amish quilts. The eastern settlements are older than those in the West, so Amish quilts from Pennsylvania can be traced to an earlier period than those from Ohio or Indiana. It also appears fair to suggest that there was greater wealth among the Lancaster County Amish than those in the Midwest. It seems likely that many Lancaster County women bought fabric for the express purpose of making quilts. Center Diamond patterns, for instance, require larger pieces of fabric than would be left as scraps from making clothing. The Pennsylvania communities were more economically stable than were the newer communities settling in the Midwest. The financial instability that came from moving to new areas was reflected in the more common use of clothing scraps in the quilts made by midwestern women. Frugality, as well as the limited accessibility of fabric stores, also accounts for the popularity of certain quilt patterns. Along with smaller pieces, midwestern quilts also boasted more lively colors.

*This funeral procession depicts the support of the community for its members even in death. These buggies have just left the funeral service held at the home of the deceased, and are on their way to a family grave plot where the body will be laid to rest.*

## More Borrowing in the Midwest

The distances between midwestern Amish settlements were greater than in Pennsylvania. So the Amish visited less with each other and had greater interaction with their "English" (the Amish term for people who are not in their church) neighbors. With that increased outside influence, the midwestern Amish adopted more daring patterns, borrowing some from neighbors and reworking old standard patterns. Consequently there is a broader spread of patterns and colors from these more farflung communities than from the more densely populated eastern settlements. But no matter their geographic origin, antique Amish quilts possess an energy that is rooted in a complex milieu of diversity and conformity, of restriction and freedom.

# Center Diamond or Diamond in Square

*10. Detail of Plate 12 on facing page.*

*The suggestion of quilt designs are found all around the farm. Here the standing wheat creates the Diamond in Square, the sheaves the quilting stitches.*

The first permanent settlement of Amish in America was in Lancaster County, Pennsylvania. Here, within the strict boundaries of Amish culture, the art of quilting flourished.

One of the oldest and plainest Amish quilt patterns is the Center Diamond, or Diamond in Square, found almost exclusively in Lancaster County quilts. In fact, this design, when discovered in other areas, can often be traced to Lancaster roots.

The pattern is very simple. A large square, made of one central fabric and tipped on its side, forms the diamond. Large triangles fill in the corners to create another square, which is then outlined by one or more borders. Borders may be broken by the addition of corner blocks. The number of colors used may be only two or as many as five.

The fact that such large sections of unbroken fabric are required for this pattern indicates fabrics were likely purchased expressly for use in a particular quilt. By contrast, many other Amish quilt patterns require small patches of fabric and can therefore accommodate scraps left over from other home sewing projects, or salvageable portions of worn-out clothing — a reflection of a frugal lifestyle.

It is difficult to decide what is more outstanding about this quilt — the bold pattern, or the quilting. Center Diamond quilts, with their large open spaces, are usually lavishly quilted with tight, tiny stitches. They are often quilted in dark thread, creating a soft, subtle design on the deep, rich colors of the quilt top surface.

Quilting designs vary, but the central diamond generally has some sort of large, dominant design. Frequently this is a large eight-pointed star inside a feather wreath, or a series of wreaths, the central one filled with small diamonds or cross-hatching. Narrow inner borders, if they are present, may be quilted with rambling grapevines, the pumpkin seed pattern or other narrow designs.

The wide outer borders repeat the generous quilting with elegant curved feathers, ferns, some floral patterns, baskets and other graceful patterns. Corners, especially where blocks are set in, may contain a new and different design rather than continuing the border pattern around the corner.

Although few quilts are signed and dated, careful observation may reveal initials or a date discreetly quilted among the graceful lines of the quilting design.

*12. Center Diamond, dated 1914. Wool, 78 x 77. Lancaster Co., Pennsylvania. The People's Place, Intercourse, Pennsylvania. The date and quilter's initials are beautifully quilted above and beside the overflowing fruit basket in one corner.*

*13. Center Diamond, c. 1900. Wool, 73 x 73. Lancaster Co., Pennsylvania. Joy Glick Hess.*

*14. Diamond in Square, 1935-36. Wool, 77 x 77. Lancaster Co., Pennsylvania. Collection of Catherine H. Anthony.*

**15.** *Center Diamond, c. 1915-20. Wool, 80 x 80. Lancaster Co., Pennsylvania. Rebecca Haarer. This quilt was sent to LaGrange Co., Indiana as a relief gift following the Palm Sunday tornados of 1965.*

**16.** *Center Diamond, 1910. Wool, 74 x 76. Lancaster Co., Pennsylvania. Ron and Marilyn Kowaleski, Grant St. Antiques, Lancaster, Pennsylvania.*

17. Center Diamond, dated 1903. Wool, 77 x 77. Lancaster Co., Pennsylvania. William B. Wigton.

18. Center Diamond with Sunshine and Shadow, 1920. Cotton, 75 x 75. Lancaster Co., Pennsylvania. Ron and Marilyn Kowaleski, Grant St. Antiques, Lancaster, Pennsylvania.

19. Center Diamond, c. 1920. Wool (cashmere), 76 x 74. Lancaster Co., Pennsylvania. Privately owned. The maker of this quilt filled nearly the entire center diamond with a series of feather wreaths.

16

**20.** *Center Diamond, 1910-20. Cotton, 72 x 75. Lancaster Co., Pennsylvania. The People's Place, Intercourse, Pennsylvania. Note the unusual use of bright orange in this Lancaster quilt.*

**21.** *Center Diamond, c. 1920. Cotton, 80 x 80. Lancaster Co., Pennsylvania. Jay M. and Susen E. Leary.*

**22.** *Center Diamond, 1925. Wool, 75 x 75. Lancaster Co., Pennsylvania. Collection of Catherine H. Anthony. This quilt shows some of the more common quilting motifs for the Center Diamond pattern.*

**23.** *Sawtooth Diamond, 1911-12. Wool, 87 x 87. Leola, Lancaster Co., Pennsylvania. Collection of Catherine H. Anthony. Note the exquisite feather quilting on the inside border and the tiny diamonds in the triangles surrounding the center square.*

**24.** *Sawtooth Center Diamond, c. 1915. Wool, 77 x 79. Lancaster Co., Pennsylvania. Privately owned. Piecing the tiny triangles and fitting them on the edge of the squares required mathematical precision and planning. This quilter had different solutions for different corners.*

**25.** *Sawtooth Center Diamond, c. 1920s. Wool, challis, 82 x 82. Lancaster Co., Pennsylvania. Paul and Lorraine Wenrich. Note the careful planning used in execution of the sawtooth pattern. Triangles in opposite corners mirror each other.*

**26.** *Sawtooth Diamond, c. 1910-15. Wool, 86 x 86. Lancaster Co., Pennsylvania. William B. Wigton.*

# Sunshine and Shadow

27. *Sunshine and Shadaow, c. 1925-30. Wool, crepe, rayon, cotton, 82 x 84. Lancaster Co., Pennsylvania. William B. Wigton. Effective blending of colors in varying shades in this quilt, which also appears on the cover, add to its drama. Colors are those often used in Amish clothing. A rose motif quilting design fills the border.*

*Life is full of sunshine and shadows. Death and life exist side by side in the Amish community where birth and old age are equally respected.*

There is a striking, almost shocking quality to the Sunshine and Shadow Quilt. Its association with a people of a quiet and subdued lifestyle seems paradoxical. Yet this quilt pattern embodies the spirit of joy and vibrance in the life of an Amish family.

Sunshine and Shadow gets its name from the light and dark effect created by the harmonizing and juxtaposition of a large variety of bold solid colors. The result may be a subtle blending of light to dark or a dramatic opposition of the two.

The Sunshine and Shadow pattern was done largely in Lancaster County, Pennsylvania, but spread to the Midwest when Amish settlements were established there. Therefore, the earliest Sunshine and Shadow quilts are likely Pennsylvania quilts while later ones may be from any Amish area.

This is a simple pattern, consisting of small squares of fabric sewn together and contained by one or several borders. The squares are arranged by color to form a series of brightly colored expanding diamonds. Sometimes the squares are tipped on their sides to form a pattern of squares.

The Sunshine and Shadow quilt traditionally has a wide outer border. Inner borders may or may not be present. Borders may be plain or contain corner blocks.

Because small squares constitute a large part of this quilt, it fits the principle of frugality practiced among the Amish. Most Amish clothes are handmade, often by the women of the household. The scraps left over from these projects could be cut for use in such a quilt. The small pieces required could also come from the still sturdy portions of worn-out clothing.

Quilting on this pattern is lavished on the borders. Here feathers are one of the most common motifs but other full designs are also used. The center squares are often quilted near the seams or simply cross-hatched in diagonal lines. Occasionally a more elaborate stitching like the clamshell design is used on each tiny square. Inner borders usually have their own quilting design the same width as the border itself.

The Sunshine and Shadow arrangement of squares worked with printed fabrics rather than plain, may be called Trip Around the World and is often done by non-Amish women. It is the solid fabrics and the wide borders of the Sunshine and Shadow quilt that make it distinctive and traditionally Amish.

**29.** *Sunshine and Shadow, c. 1930. Cotton, wool, 81 x 84. Lancaster Co., Pennsylvania. Jay M. and Susen E. Leary. A wide range of colors make this quilt dance.*

**30.** *Sunshine and Shadow, dated 1926. Cotton, 72 x 80. Mifflin Co., Pennsylvania. William and Connie Hayes. The corners of this quilt are less well planned than the center so that the pattern of concentric diamonds breaks near the outside.*

**31.** *Sunshine and Shadow, c. 1930. Wool and cotton, 86 x 86. Lancaster Co., Pennsylvania. Collection of Catherine H. Anthony. A well-planned gradation of colors creates a magical light and dark interplay in this quilt.*

**32.** *Sunshine and Shadow, early 1940s. Wool challis, crepe, 84 x 82. Lancaster Co., Pennsylvania. Paul and Lorraine Wenrich.*

**33.** *Sunshine and Shadow, c. 1900. Wool, 84 x 84. Lancaster Co., Pennsylvania. Jay M. and Susen E. Leary. The squares in this quilt are tipped on their sides which creates a series of concentric squares rather than diamonds.*

**34.** *Sunshine and Shadow, 1940s. Cotton, crepe, 88 x 86. Lancaster Co., Pennsylvania. The People's Place, Intercourse, Pennsylvania. A rambling rose pattern is quilted on the outside borders of this later quilt.*

**35.** *Sunshine and Shadow, c. 1930. Cotton, wool, crepe, 86 x 86. Lancaster Co., Pennsylvania. Jay M. and Susen E. Leary. This quiltmaker combined the Sunshine and Shadow pattern with the Center Diamond to create a different look.*

*Though simple, Amish houses are warm and friendly. Attention is given to cleanliness and order.*

# Color Among the Amish

Probably the most distinctive quality about Amish quilts is their color. Other quilters from the past would on occasion use exclusively solid fabrics. But Amish women consistently used only solid colors for their quilts. Most antique quilts are made from fabric scraps, usually left over from other sewing projects. Since much Amish clothing, especially women's dresses, men's shirts, and children's clothing, has traditionally been made at home, it is the fabric left from these handmade dresses and shirts that create the vivid, deep colors found in Amish quilts.

Amish clothing at a quick glance seems dark and somber because of its heavy use of black. But children's clothing and young women's dresses are gaily colored blues, greens, purples, pinks and dark reds. Although the styles are conservative (children wear miniature models of adult clothing), the colors are bold and bright. The colors, it seems, match the children's energies.

## "Naive" Color Combinations

Amish quilts are also generally spoken of as "dark." However, there are few quilts as daring and bold in color as those made by the Amish. How can this seeming paradox

be explained? Amish quiltmakers, because of their limited access to color and fashion trends, work in a nearly uninhibited color world. Most children in the larger society begin early in their lives to subconsciously develop a color sense. Their socks match their pants; their pants match their shirt; their sweaters are coordinated. All this takes place in homes where carpets, draperies, and walls are synchronized with accessories and furnishings.

In an Amish setting, one style of clothing is worn and only part of its color changes from day to day. One never need worry about whether one's pink dress matches one's black stockings and black shoes. Most Amish homes do not contain upholstered furniture, their walls are generally painted a solid blue or green, and carpets, where found, are often hand-woven rag rugs. This lack of color consciousness among the Amish leaves them completely open to the possible use of fabrics from their scrap bag.

Amish women were not told that color hues vary depending on their reference point. But they could see—and feel—it happening. Numerous quilts were pieced without the maker's knowledge of the science of what she was doing. She saw it and knew inherently that the two colors brought out the best in each other. For example, many antique Amish quilts have touches of black and red, two choices which add spark to nearly any color scheme. Amish women simply recognized it as a pleasing combination. Their approach to color was new, fresh, and followed gut-level instincts. Perhaps that is why these quilts have such wide appeal. Everyone's creative sense knows when something is correct, but too often the "modern" person knows too much to make these free decisions.

## Clothing Colors Used Primarily

Among the Old Order Amish there were and are stipulations about clothing colors. The more conservative groups of Eastern Pennsylvania avoid red, red-orange, orange, and yellow. But burgundy hues are permitted. Amish groups in Mifflin County, Pennsylvania, use many bright, gaudy colors including yellows. Midwestern Amish also tend to allow bright and varied clothing colors.

Occasionally a "stray" color appears in an antique Amish quilt. One Amish woman explained how these color exceptions may have happened: midwestern Amish women often bought fabrics from peddlers who went from home to home with their wares. A good peddler learned to know his territory and how to market his merchandise. He knew what kinds of fabrics appealed to his Amish clients and made bundles of those fabrics offering them at a bargain rate. But among the desirables he might place some pieces that were slow movers. One Amish woman wanted a bundle of fabrics that contained a piece of bright red cloth. Knowing that this particular color was out of her domain, she explained to the peddler that she would like the bundle but with an exchange for the red. Apparently having had trouble moving the red elsewhere, he refused to swap. So she purchased, along with her needs, a piece that she could use only in a secondary function. This bright red cloth became quilt fabric.

## Some Quilt Fabrics Purchased

Not all old quilts are made from scraps. Large sections of fabrics used for backings and borders needed to be purchased. But the principle of frugality is strong among these people. So remnant shopping and bargain hunting for fabrics was likely common and would account for some of the exceptional colors used. Backings were sometimes printed fabrics even though prints are seldom permitted for clothing.

These old quilts delight and surprise the viewer with their vibrance and lasting beauty. They bridge the gap from a separate people to the modern world. Their beauty, though perhaps understood in different ways by each group, is loved and appreciated by both.

*Vivid juxtaposition of color in the Amish world is common. Somber dress intensifies the spritely colors for which Amish quilts are well known.*

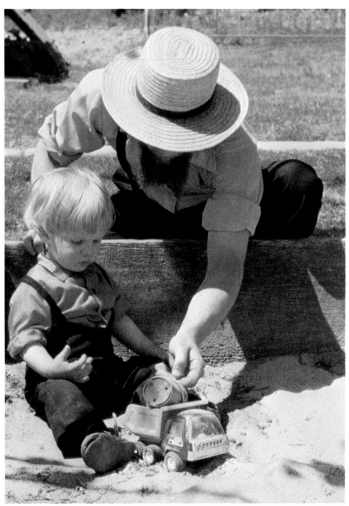

*Many Amish are employed at home on the farm. As a result, parents and children spend more time together than in families where one or both parents drive to work.*

# Bars

**39.** *Bars, c. 1890-1900. Wool, 72 x 87. Lancaster Co., Pennsylvania. William B. Wigton.*

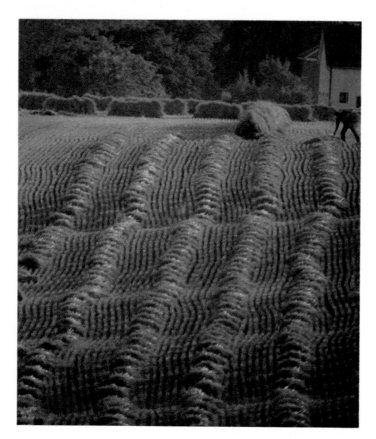

Bars is a pattern of stark simplicity — straight vertical pieces surrounded by a border. There may be only two colors used alternately or an assortment of colors differing in each vertical bar.

Although it does appear among the midwestern Amish, the Bars pattern is a simple, plain one and was made largely among the Pennsylvania Amish. These quilts usually have wide borders covered with generous quilting, typical of Pennsylvania Amish quilts.

The most basic Bars quilt lacks any ornamentation other than the quilting designs, but variations of the Bars pattern exemplify the spirit of adventure and exploration found among this outwardly austere people.

The Split Bars variation adds interest by splitting the larger bands of color with additional narrow bands. Some quilters added a pieced inner border, while others created patterns within the bars themselves. The Wild Goose Chase pattern, for example, has a series of triangles ascending and descending the bars, giving the illusion of birds in flight. And a collection of Nine Patch blocks can be stacked inside the bars to give a more interesting design.

The quilting designs on a Bars quilt more than adequately compensates for what may seem to be cold, stark piecing. The entire inner section of bars is sometimes treated as a whole and quilted in continuous lines of small even diamonds or some graceful, flowing design. Or each bar may be quilted in its own motif, giving a sampling of many different quilting designs. The open borders create a challenge for any avid quilter to use an abundance of feathers, cables, or other delicately stitched patterns.

It is not possible to make definitive statements about the inspiration for such a quilt design. However, it is likely that a people so close to the earth would be inclined to incorporate patterns of the field and the garden into other areas of life. One only needs observe a few of the meticulous gardens and fields of the Old Order Amish to see their pride in strong, straight lines. Plowed furrows in long even stretches, horizontal slats on wooden fences, or tobacco barns with opened vents could have provided the impetus for an Amish woman to create the Bars quilt.

*Harvest is a time for thanksgiving. The Bars quilt pattern is reflected in this evening photo and the quilting motif is parallel to the rows of stubble.*

*41.* Bars, 1910-20. Cotton, 78 x 73. Lancaster Co., Pennsylvania. The People's Place, Intercourse, Pennsylvania.

**42.** *Bars Variation (Nine Patch), c. 1905. Wool, flannel back, 90 x 68. Elkhart Co., Indiana. Rebecca Haarer.*

**43.** *Bars, c. 1870-80. Wool, cotton, 84 x 66. Mifflin Co., Pennsylvania. William B. Wigton. Unlike most Pennsylvania quilts, this one does not have a border. Note the extravagant quilting designs used throughout the quilt top.*

**44.** *Bars, c. 1900. Wool, 79 x 69. Lancaster Co., Pennsylvania. Orpha M. Hege. The border quilting design contains baskets filled with fruit. Pears and apples are quilted between baskets.*

**45.** *Wild Goose Chase in Bars, c. 1880-90. Cotton, 69 x 79. Mifflin Co., Pennsylvania. William B. Wigton.*

**46.** *Wild Goose Chase, Bars Variation, c. 1915. Wool, 84 x 66. Lancaster Co., Pennsylvania. Rebecca Haarer. This quilt traveled from Pennsylvania to Indiana in a relief box to victims of the Palm Sunday tornados in 1965.*

47. *Split Bars, 1933. Cotton, 80 x 80. Lancaster Co., Pennsylvania. Collection of Catherine H. Anthony. The rose quilting design used on the borders is also repeated in the bars design.*

48. *Bars, c. 1930. Cotton, 83 x 85. Lancaster Co., Pennsylvania. Jay M. and Susen E. Leary. An inside border with pieced diamonds adds interest to this design. Pineapples are quilted among feathers on the exterior borders.*

49. *Bars Variation, c. 1900-10. Cotton and wool, 73 x 63. Iowa. Judi Boisson Antique American Quilts, New York.*

*50-51. Sampler, dated 1926. Cotton, 71 x 82. Mifflin Co., Pennsylvania. Judi Boisson Antique American Quilts, New York. This rare quilt is a sampler pattern on one side with bars on the reverse side (see below). Quilting is a simple cross-hatch design throughout.*

# Multiple Patch Quilts

*52. Blockwork, c. 1910. Glazed cotton, 67 x 73. Holmes Co., Ohio. Judi Boisson Antique American Quilts, New York. This pattern looks like a collection of miniature center diamond blocks collected and set together into one quilt.*

This grouping covers a range of quilts from the simple One Patch pattern to the more complex Double Nine Patch, with variations on all these designs.

The One Patch is just what its name implies—a quilt made up of a series of single patches sewn together in a random or an organized fashion. The Four Patch is a series of blocks consisting of small patches in groups of four. The Double Four Patch uses a set of two four-patch blocks pieced with two solid patches the size of the quartet patch to form a square of four blocks. A series of these "double-four" blocks are sewn together, with sashing setting each square of four blocks apart.

The Nine Patch is the same idea worked in a series of threes. Nine small patches (three horizontal by three vertical patches) are sewn together to make a square. The Double Nine Patch uses five of these nine-square patches pieced together with four solid patches the size of the nine-patch to form a larger nine-patch combination. These large Double Nine Patches are sewn together, often separated by sashing to form the quilt top. Variations include the Four Patch in a Nine Patch, Nine Patch, or Four Patch in a Block Work.

The pattern is a simple one but the many possibilities allowed within the patches make it intriguing. Seldom are all the patches within a quilt done in the same color scheme. This multitude of color differences makes this a quilt with a sparkling potential.

Because of the small pieces and numerous color possibilities, it is an excellent pattern for a "scrap quilt." Any small snippet or scrap can be worked in at some spot.

This pattern was likely a first choice for many girls beginning their piecing skills. The simple straight lines make it easy to piece but the size and number of patches create enough challenge for a novice to tackle it with pride.

It is not only a beginner's quilt, however. The magnificent craftsmanship found in many of these quilts shows they are obviously the work of experienced and skilled hands.

*The Amish are not opposed to education but they are cautious about too much formal training, especially in consolidated schools. The interplay of light and dark blocks in this Amish school is similar to the geometry in Multiple Patch quilts.*

**54.** *Double Nine Patch, c. 1930. Cotton, 83 x 82. Lancaster Co., Pennsylvania. Jay M. and Susen E. Leary. A pieced inner border of bright colors adds interest to this pattern.*

**56.** *Four in Block Work, c. 1930. Cotton, rayon, 73 x 86. Mifflin Co., Pennsylvania. William B. Wigton. The framing of the four patch blocks is reminiscent of the Center Diamond pattern.*

**55.** *One Patch, c. 1915. Cotton, worsted wool, 76 x 69. Medford, Wisconsin. Judi Boisson Antique American Quilts, New York. Although this is a very simple pieced pattern, the borders of the quilt are elegantly quilted with fiddlehead ferns.*

**58.** *Double Four Patch, c. 1920. Cotton sateen, 68 x 78. Mifflin Co., Pennsylvania. William B. Wigton. Tiny initials are embroidered on the border of this quilt.*

**57.** *Double Four Patch, dated 1913. Wool, 83 x 71. Elkhart Co., Indiana. Joseph M. B. Sarah.*

**59.** *Four Patch-Nine Patch, c. 1920. Cotton sateen, 71 x 80. Mifflin Co., Pennsylvania. Judi Boisson Antique American Quilts, New York.*

**60.** *Four Patch in Nine Patch, c. 1920-25. Cotton sateen, 83 x 77. Mifflin Co., Pennsylvania. Reed Hayes. Black and pink squares mark a grid across the quilt top.*

**61.** *Four Patch and Triangles Combination, c. 1910. Cotton, 78 x 84. Mifflin Co., Pennsylvania. William B. Wigton. Four patches with triangles form diagonal lines that shoot across the quilt top. A strong border contains the vibrance of this design.*

**62.** *Nine Patch, c. 1900. Wool, mohair, 70 x 80. Mifflin Co., Pennsylvania. William and Connie Hayes. Careful placement of blue squares creates a rectangle in the center of the quilt. Red squares repeat the pattern in an outer rectangle.*

**63.** *Four in Split Nine Patch, c. 1925. Cotton, 67 x 76. Mifflin Co., Pennsylvania. William B. Wigton. Four-patch blocks are matched with rectangular shapes to achieve this interesting block work.*

**64.** *Nine Patch, 1890. Wool, 77 x 84. Belleville, Mifflin Co., Pennsylvania. Ron and Marilyn Kowaleski, Grant St. Antiques, Lancaster, Pennsylvania. A sawtooth inner border frames the nine-patch blocks.*

**65.** *Double Nine Patch, c. 1925-1930. Wool, wool-rayon, 74 x 76. Lancaster Co., Pennsylvania. William B. Wigton. Triangles form an unusual inner border for this otherwise typical design.*

**66.** *Double Nine Patch, c. 1915. Cotton, 46 x 78. Holmes Co., Ohio. William B. Wigton. The unusual dimensions of this quilt suggest that it was probably made for a hired man's bed.*

**67.** *Nine Patch Variation, c. 1930. Cotton, 64 x 76. Mifflin Co., Pennsylvania. William and Connie Hayes.*

**68.** *Double Nine Patch, c. 1910. Cotton, 61 x 79. Collected LaGrange Co., Indiana. Rebecca Haarer. Triangles surrounding the sashed nine patch blocks are pieced at several places indicating that the maker was likely using some scraps.*

**69.** *Double Nine Patch, c. 1910. Cotton, wool, 68 x 74. Collected LaGrange Co., Indiana. Rebecca Haarer. This is truly a scrap quilt! Even the tiny squares in the nine-patch blocks are sometimes pieced.*

**70.** *Nine Patch in Block Work, c. 1910. Cotton, 69 x 79. Mifflin Co., Pennsylvania. William B. Wigton. Careful placement of pink patches create a chain pattern on the quilt surface. This is very similar to the Single Irish Chain quilt in photo #72.*

**71.** *Nine Patch in Block Work, c. 1920. Cotton, wool, 74 x 83. Mifflin Co., Pennsylvania. William and Connie Hayes. Only one block in this quilt deviates from the norm of using four pink squares in the borders of the nine-patch blocks.*

# Irish Chain

**72.** *Single Irish Chain, c. 1920. Cotton, sateen, 64 x 70. Wayne Co., Ohio. William B. Wigton.*

*These three girls are watching a game of baseball played on a Sunday afternoon in the neighbor's meadow. The fence pattern reminds one of an Irish Chain quilt.*

Here is a quilt with simple elegance — clear, sharp lines with ample space for generous quilting. The Irish Chain pattern can be pieced as a single row of blocks, a double row, or a triple row: the category is determined by the number of blocks creating the "chain" that runs diagonally or vertically through the quilt.

The single Irish Chain quilt can be constructed rather simply by making a series of simple Nine-Patch blocks in two colors. These are then tipped on their corners and sewn together alternately with solid squares of the same color to form the Single Irish Chain. Other variations of the pattern are much more complicated, requiring very careful placement of colors to create the chain effect.

The double and triple chain varieties often combine a bit of applique with the piecework. These patterns are sewn together so that a multiple patch is alternated with a solid patch of fabric the same size as the multiple patch. To achieve a consistent chain effect, small squares must be added to the corners of these solid patches. It is often easiest to applique those additional squares on top rather than trying to piece a right-angled corner.

The solid squares between the chain pattern as well as the typically wide borders on these quilts provide ample space for the outstanding quilting skills evident in Amish quilts. Curved, flowing quilting lines provide a contrast for the angles created by the pieced chain.

While the colors and fabrics used in Amish Irish Chain quilts make them distinctive, this is not a pattern unique to Amish quiltmakers. Irish Chain quilts were made by quilters in general. At some point, an Amish woman likely borrowed the pattern from a neighbor or friend and from there it probably circulated among Amish quilters.

*74. Triple Irish Chain, c. 1920. Cotton, 72 x 88. Mifflin Co., Pennsylvania. William B. Wigton.*

75. *Double Irish Chain, dated 1927. Cotton, 73 x 74. LaGrange Co., Indiana. Faye and Don Walters.*

76. *Triple Irish Chain, c. 1915-20. Wool, 76½ x 76½. Lancaster Co., Pennsylvania. Joseph M. B. Sarah.*

77. *Triple Irish Chain, 1864. Cashmere, cotton, 68 x 88. Lancaster Co., Pennsylvania. Anna Lois Umble.*

**78.** *Double Irish Chain, c. 1920. Wool, 77 x 79. Lancaster Co., Pennsylvania. Jay M. and Susen E. Leary.*

**79.** *Triple Irish Chain with embroidered Baskets, c. 1930-40. Cotton, 72 x 76. Belleville, Mifflin Co., Pennsylvania. Romaine S. Sala.*

**80.** *Triple Irish Chain Variation, dated 1940. Cotton, 77 x 81. Collected Holmes Co., Ohio. Judi Boisson Antique American Quilts, New York.*

**81.** *Triple Irish Chain Variation, dated 1944. Cotton, 78 x 79. Tuseawras Co., Ohio. Judi Boisson Antique American Quilts, New York.*

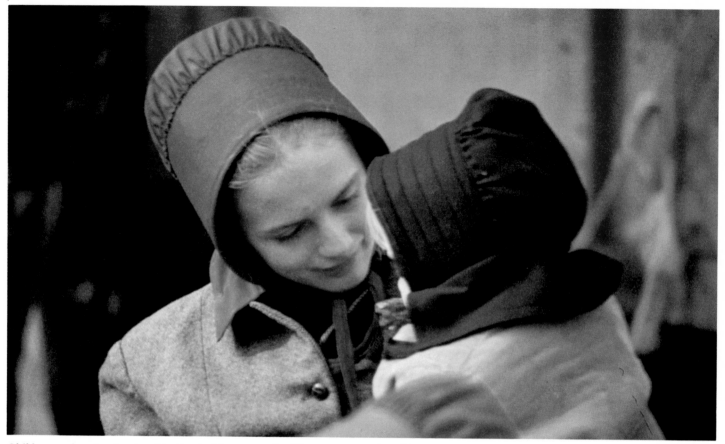

*Children are loved and enjoyed in the Amish community. They grow up eating, drinking, playing and working "Amishness" and usually join the church as young adults.*

# Quilts in the Life Cycle

A people who live from the land know well its seasons and changes. And their own day-to-day lives flow in rhythm with the earth's movement.

## The Earth Gives

Spring is the time for planting fields, gardens, and flower beds. Housecleaning gets underway with the women scrubbing the house from top to bottom, airing the mattresses, beating the rugs, wiping walls and ceilings, washing windows to a sparkle, and emptying and cleaning cupboards and drawers. With warmer weather comes vigor for these projects. There is a freshness in the air indoors and out. Lawns are raked free of debris and primped and prepared for the burst of color promised by newly planted flower beds.

Field work begins and ends with the sun. Men and those children no longer in school spend long days standing on the plow behind a team of horses. Their reward? The smell and texture of newly turned earth!

Summer and the closing of school bring extra hands to help hoe the corn, top tobacco, and cut and bale hay before the rain comes. It is a rushed time, but rich in the earth's plenty. There are strawberries to pick, peas to pod, beans to

shell and corn to be husked. There are new potatoes and tender asparagus to be collected. Cantaloupes, watermelons and fresh fruits offer themselves for snacks and desserts. Not only is there enough to fill summertime tables, but all the fruits have been planted in excess so as to be preserved for the winter months.

Fall comes and with it the children's return to school, the last of the harvest and quieter days on the farm. Fall housecleaning sweeps away the summer's clutter. Window screens are replaced with storm windows; hay mows and corn cribs are stacked full; silos burst with food for cattle during cold months. And when the days become shorter and winter's nip is in the air, butchering day arrives. Meats are canned, smoked, or frozen for use throughout the cold months.

## The Earth Grows Quiet

Winter is a time for repairs and maintenance around the farm. There are fewer demands from the fields and garden, so the farm family fix their energies on other projects. It is during these slower times when the earth is frozen and silent that many women turn to quiltmaking.

It would be misleading to say that all Amish women enjoy quilting. For some it is as natural as housecleaning and gardening. For others it is tedious work and something they simply prefer not to do. But for many women, it is a fulfilling undertaking learned at the elbows of their mothers and kept alive by tradition and their own enthusiasm.

# Growing Up

Discipine is strict in Amish families and is evidenced in the children's ability to sit quietly during the three hour Sunday morning church services. Children are treated firmly but not harshly. They learn early to take responsibility around the farm and are often given specific chores in both house and farm work. One of the skills often taught young children is to handstitch small patches together for a quilt top. Not only do they learn a specific skill but these children are at the same time being taught perseverance, patience, and a lack of idleness. Young girls eventually learn to embroider and finally to make their own clothing. Along the way, most girls follow the example of the older women in their lives and also learn to quilt.

# Families Wrapped in Love — and Quilts

Part of the magic of quilting is that it can be done in groups. Fun and visiting happen around the quilting frame. Young Amish women, like teenagers everywhere, dream about their futures. For most the choices are clearcut—marriage, family, and a carrying on of their way of life. It is not unusual for an Amish girl in her early teens to begin making several quilts in anticipation of her marriage and children.

Among the Amish, large families are received with great joy. And in preparation for these gifts from God, expectant mothers and grandmothers turn to making crib quilts. Most women are not employed outside of the home. They view mothering and caring for their homes as honorable and worthwhile positions. The responsibility of raising children in a God-fearing manner is foremost in the minds of these parents.

How do Amish women, with their large families and basic, back-to-earth lifestyle, find time to quilt? Time is a relative concept. Many Amish homesteads operate as extended families with two or three generations living under one roof. Although each family lives separately, there is daily interaction between generations. Consequently, both moral support and physical help flow in all directions. And children, although the primary care of their parents, relate closely to grandparents whose lifestyle and values match what they see at home.

Parents work hard at establishing "Amish" values in their offspring. However, as children become teenagers, they are gently freed of parental ties and the choice to leave or stay within the community is one that must be made by each individual. For many young adults marrying and joining the church happen at about the same time. Both are lifetime commitments supported by family and church.

The Amish are, in general, a restrained people. They show little overt emotion or affection. But in place of kisses and embraces, Amish women demonstrate their love through their offerings of quilts and favorite foods, both lovingly prepared and assembled. Many mothers make quilts to present to their sons and daughters at their marriages.

Some quilts seem to have been intended as heirlooms and show quilts, for use on beds only on Sundays and when company was coming. Both the memories of their owners and the condition of these bedcovers bear out this intent. These quilts are in such excellent condition that it seems they were never used. Perhaps the makers knew that the love invested in each tiny quilting stitch would serve as long time testament to that affection.

# Quilting Belongs to All Ages

Growing old is not a tragedy in the Amish world. Age carries the respect of wisdom and the elderly are cared for

*The Amish care for their own elderly instead of leaving that to Social Security. Additions are built onto the original farmhouse to make room for two or three generations.*

with dignity. Aging family members are nursed at home unless they require hospitalization. Around the farm there are jobs that can keep men busy even though their strength and health may be failing. There is nearly always a son or grandson for them to assist.

Women stay involved in domestic chores and childcare until it becomes physically impossible for them. Here again quilting fits into the life cycle. Old age and new blood work elbow to elbow on a project that symbolizes Amish life. One generation learns from the next with the knowledge that time goes on and with it the cycle of life. Death is seen as a natural part of having lived. When one becomes old, death is the doorway to a new life and a stepping stone for the next generation.

# Log Cabin

A favorite with quiltmakers in general, the Log Cabin also thrived among Amish quilters. Its possibilities are almost infinite. There are Barn Raising, Courthouse Steps, Straight Furrows, and Pineapple or Windmill Blades variations. And each of those can be made with solid borders, pieced borders, or no border at all.

The Log Cabin quilt is often a scrap quilt. Its narrow "log"-shaped pieces in varying lengths could accommodate many scraps that were not large enough for other patterns. Perhaps this is why so many Log Cabin quilts flourish in so many diverse constructions.

Assembly of this quilt is straightforward. It begins with a center square upon which the "logs" are stacked. The first is the length of the square. The block is then rotated one-quarter turn and the next log (the length of the square plus the previous log) is added. This continues with varying numbers of logs to form the basic log cabin patch.

Patches are often arranged with light fabrics on one half of the block and dark fabrics on the other half, which when sewn together, produce a larger pattern on the quilt top.

*84. Log Cabin — Diagonal Furrows Variation, c. 1900-10. Wool, 66 x 78. Mifflin Co. Pennsylvania. William and Connie Hayes.*

The visual images are apparent. One can see the sun streaming through the rafters of a barn under construction. Straight furrows are sharp and clear and the dark patches conjure up images of rich, dark soil waiting to burst forth with harvest. The tiny steps of the logs create the Courthouse Steps, and the Windmill Blades variation seems to spin as easily as the windmill pumping water on an Amish farm.

Log Cabin quilts are one of the exceptions to the general rule of elaborate quilting on Amish quilts. These quilts are sometimes quilted only on the borders, sometimes not at all. In some cases the quilt top, lining, and backing are connected in the piecing process. The blocks are then sewn together, eliminating the functional need for quilting. In other cases, quilts are "tied" or "knotted" (tacked with heavy string at regular intervals) rather than quilted. That may have been done because the narrow width of the logs creates the problem of having to quilt through a seam allowance, thus making quilting less pleasurable and less fine. When Log Cabin patterns are quilted, the stitching is usually minimal in the pieced part of the quilt and more abundant on the borders.

*Mutual aid is a way of life for the Amish. Barn raisings are common in Amish settlements, both in the actual construction of barns and in the Log Cabin quilt pattern.*

**86.** *Log Cabin, c. 1890-1900. Wool, 82 x 84. Mifflin Co., Pennsylvania. William B. Wigton. A strong contrast in colors makes the barn raising design in this quilt very obvious. The pieced borders continue the theme of narrow strips.*

**87.** *Log Cabin — Courthouse Steps Variation, c. 1910-20. Cotton, wool, 68 x 76. Collected LaGrange Co., Indiana. Rebecca Haarer. Borders on this quilt contain beautifully quilted feather designs.*

**88.** *Log Cabin — Courthouse Steps Variation, c. 1880-90. Wool, 71 x 67. Collected Indiana. Judi Boisson Antique American Quilts, New York. A pieced border along two sides of the quilt provides extra width and adds interest to the design.*

**89.** *Log Cabin, c. 1880. Wool and cotton, 79 x 71. Lancaster Co., Pennsylvania. Naomi E. Yoder. Tiny initials of the man for whom this quilt was made are cross-stitched in the center square of the bottom left block.*

**90.** *Pineapple, c. 1920-30. Cotton, 75 x 82. Ohio. Judi Boisson Antique American Quilts, New York. Very careful use of fabric creates a double pattern in this quilt. Fine quilting as well as the addition of the saw-tooth border at top and bottom show this to be the work of a master.*

**91.** *Pineapple or Windmill Blades, c. 1880-90. Wool, 70 x 79. Collected Mifflin Co., Pennsylvania. The Darwin D. Bearley Collection.*

**93.** *Log Cabin — Barn Raising Variation, c. 1920. Cotton, wool, crepe, 78 x 78. Lancaster Co., Pennsylvania. Jay M. and Susen E. Leary.*

**92.** *Log Cabin — Barn Raising Variation, c. 1890. Wool, 80 x 80. Mifflin Co., Pennsylvania. The Darwin D. Bearley Collection. A very carefully planned group of log cabin patches have been tipped on their sides in assembly to create a pattern of concentric squares.*

**94.** *Log Cabin — Barn Raising Variation, 1920. Cotton, wool, 68 x 70. Topeka, La-Grange Co., Indiana. Rebecca Haarer. Light and dark patches appear to be mixed in this bedcover but the quilter has successfully a-chieved an overall barn raising effect. This top was pieced by Sarah Miller for her son Jacob and quilted by Sarah and Jacob's bride.*

**95.** *Log Cabin — Barn Raising Variation, 1932. Cotton, 86 x 76. Emma, LaGrange Co., Indiana. Rebecca Haarer. Bright yellow contrasts with other colors to create the barn-raising effect. The entire quilt is covered with tiny quilted diamonds.*

**96.** *Log Cabin — Barn Raising Variation, dated 1920. Cotton, wool, 68 x 70. Topeka, LaGrange Co., Indiana. Rebecca Haarer. The unusual addition of a pieced inner border creates a nice double framing effect.*

# Double T

It is often difficult to document how patterns were developed or named. The Double T, however, looks like what it is called — a T that mirrors itself in two directions. Perhaps this particular pattern began as a Nine Patch (see the center of the Double T patch).

This pattern is seldom found among Amish quilts of Pennsylvania. It is a Midwestern quilt pattern, perhaps learned by an Amish woman from a neighbor. There seems to have been much more borrowing by the Midwestern Amish of patterns from outside their community; at least, these Amish used many more patterns than did the Pennsylvania Amish. Perhaps the same spirit of adventure and necessity that allowed Amish families to move West is reflected in their more experimental attitudes in quiltmaking.

Quilting is an integral part of most Amish quilts. This pattern is no exception. Borders and open blocks between piecework encourage the abundance of stitching that helps make these quilts the masterpieces they are.

**97.** *Double T, c. 1920. Cotton, 80 x 70. Northern Indiana. Nancy Meng. A triple inside border and generous quilting add to the beauty of the quilt.*

*Detail of above quilt.*
*Note the subtle color variations in this dichromatic quilt.*

# Stars

**99.** *Broken Star, c. 1920-30. Cotton, 85 x 85. Ohio. Judi Boisson Antique American Quilts, New York. The use of the tiny nine patch blocks bring together the corners of the triple inside border. Fiddlehead ferns are quilted throughout the border.*

*Star motifs are common in Amish quilts and handcrafts. Perhaps this intrigue with heavenly bodies stems from their day's work, beginning and ending at the bidding of the sun.*

Numerous quilt patterns deal with the heavenly bodies. Perhaps this fascination with the sky stems from the fact that so much of rural life begins and ends at the bidding of the sun.

The rising and setting sun are particularly important in an Amish home. Without electric lights, sewing is frequently done inside a window where one can reap the full benefit of the sun's light. While gas lamps provide ample light for reading or a game of checkers, the coming of darkness brings rest and the time for work to cease.

Probably the most dramatic of the star quilt patterns are the Lone Star and the Broken Star. In these, a large star seems to burst from the center of the quilt, sending light to the ends of its eight points. In the Broken Star, the additional energy of a pieced border surrounding the central star causes the pattern to appear to pulsate.

Successful construction of these quilts requires meticulous accuracy in cutting and piecing the small diamonds. A minute error will be numerously multiplied when trying to match the diamonds' corners in this magnificent quilt.

Quilting adds another striking feature to these already dramatic bedcovers. Open corners surrounding the stars and wide outer borders seem always to inspire fresh energy and imagination in quilters. This ornamental stitching adds depth and grace to the quilt.

Star quilts come in an abundance of shapes and sizes. In addition to the large star patterns there are many smaller star designs worked in a series of blocks.

One of the features that make the Amish star quilts so outstanding is their fabrics. Many of these star quilts have backgrounds of a very dark color, making the star itself seem to sparkle like the stars in a clear night sky.

Star patterns, although popular with quilters in general, seem to have been accepted and widely used by the Amish. It suggests a wonderful blending of their respect for God's creation and their love of beauty.

*101. Broken Star, c. 1925-30. Cotton, 72 x 72. Ohio. William and Connie Hayes.*

**102.** *Broken Star, c. 1930-40. Cotton, 89 x 89. Holmes Co., Ohio. Judi Boisson Antique American Quilts, New York.*

**103.** *Broken Star, dated 1938. Cotton, 90 x 90. Holmes Co., Ohio. Judi Boisson Antique American Quilts, New York.*

**104.** *Lone Star, 1921. Cotton, 74 x 68. La-Grange Co., Indiana. Rebecca Haarer. Effective use of color creates an outline of the star. Red diamonds on the points of the star add spark and vibrance.*

**105.** *Lone Star, c. 1930. Cotton, 74 x 74. Ohio. William B. Wigton. The maker of this quilt intentionally or accidentally reversed the placement of a green and yellow diamond at the widest point of this star.*

**106.** *Series of Stars, c. 1920. Cotton, wool, 78 x 78. Lancaster Co., Pennsylvania. Jay M. and Susen E. Leary.*

**107.** *Stars and Blocks, late 1920s. Cotton, 72 x 85. Holmes Co., Ohio. Collection of Catherine H. Anthony.*

**108.** *Eight Point Star, 1920s. Glazed cotton, 78 x 75. Ohio. Judi Boisson Antique American Quilts, New York.*

**109.** *Stars and Stripes, late 1920s-early 1930s. Cotton, 64 x 80. Walnut Creek, Ohio. Collection of Catherine H. Anthony.*

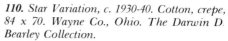

**110.** *Star Variation, c. 1930-40. Cotton, crepe, 84 x 70. Wayne Co., Ohio. The Darwin D. Bearley Collection.*

**111.** *"Star Medallion," c. 1910. Cotton, 73 x 77. Elkhart Co., Indiana. Judi Boisson Antique American Quilts, New York. Similar in concept to the Tumbling Blocks Pattern, the stars in this quilt are created from diamonds but the hexagons between stars are solid pieces.*

**112.** *String Star or Crazy Star, c. 1915-20. Cotton, wool, 81 x 80. Elkhart Co., Indiana. Joseph M. B. Sarah.*

# Jacob's Ladder

The Jacob's Ladder pattern was brought into the Amish community from outside. Its religious roots perhaps made it desirable to Amish women.

Jacob's Ladder depicts the ladder from the Old Testament story of Jacob's vision of angels ascending and descending from heaven to minister to him on earth.

Colors must be carefully arranged to execute this pattern correctly. The pattern is a series of four patch blocks and triangles arranged with light and dark fabrics to form continuous diagonals across the quilt surface.

Quilting on the pieced portion of this quilt is generally done in straight lines with more elaborate quilting on the borders.

*113. Jacob's Ladder, c. 1920. Cotton, 68 x 80. Probably LaGrange Co., Indiana. Rebecca Haarer. One isolated blue patch wandered into the making of an otherwise subdued color scheme.*

*Detail of above quilt. A single patch in a quilt that stands alone in its color selection and combination is common in old Amish quilts.*

# Plain Quilts

"Plain quilts" seems a wrong term for these vibrant bedcovers. And yet a parallel can be drawn between this pattern (or lack of it) and the Amish way of life. At first glance both seem severe and almost drab. Only careful scrutiny reveals fullness and refined simplicity.

In these bedcovers is evidence that quilts were more finely done than function alone would require. Their rich spreads of extravagant quilting go way beyond the stitches necessary to keep the top, lining, and backing intact.

Here is sheer appreciation for the skill and beauty of quilting. A woman who undertook such a project was certainly no novice with the quilting needle. Such a venture undoubtedly provided a creative outlet for her skilled hands. This channeling of creative energies into a functional object fits the Amish principles of humility, frugality, and simplicity.

*115,117. Plain, c. 1910. Cotton, 89 x 66. Reno Co., Kansas. Mrs. Mary Bontrager. Exquisite quilting covers this quilt. It is reversible (see facing page), one side being black with blue and green inside borders, the other green with blue and black inside borders.*

*Quilting motifs can be found in many aspects of rural life. This spiderweb, stretched within the pasture fence, reflects a medallion pattern frequently quilted in plain quilts.*

*118. Center Square, c. 1880. Wool, 83 x 83. Lancaster Co., Pennsylvania. Jay M. and Susen E. Leary. The pieced design and central quilting is plain but the border is elaborately quilted. The feather quilting motif ends with a tiny heart design.*

*119. Center Square, c. 1890. Wool, 78 x 84. Lancaster Co., Pennsylvania. Jay M. and Susen E. Leary.*

**120.** *Plain, or Double Inside Border, 1910. Cotton, 69 x 59. Ohio. Judi Boisson Antique American Quilts, New York. Six feather wreaths fill the interior of the quilt and fiddle-head ferns are quilted on the border.*

**121.** *Plain, c. 1900. Wool, cotton sateen, 32 x 66. Holmes Co., Ohio. William B. Wigton. This shape suggests the quilt was probably made for a hired man's bed.*

**122.** *Plain, March 31, 1946 quilted in center. Cotton, 65 x 77. Holmes Co., Ohio. Collection of Catherine H. Anthony. A bold, sharp-pieced design is softened with curved quilting lines.*

*These Amish boys have congregated on the front porch of their school. The roof was on fire earlier in the day because the wood stove fire had gotten too hot.*

*Ice skating is a wonderful winter pasttime for many Amish. It's a time to let ice hockey and crack-the-whip add some zest to cold winter afternoons.*

# Excerpts from a Grandmother's Diary

This diary represents the life of an Amish woman throughout the year. Many of the entries were first published as news items in Amish publications. Names and places were changed to protect the identities of the people involved.

"Sadie's Diary" was originally compiled by the staff of The People's Place in Intercourse, Pennsylvania where it now hangs as a wall mural.

**January 5** — Yesterday Amos Stoltzfus attended the funeral of Abner King of New York State. He died of a heart attack if he was informed right.

**January 12** — I took in the quilting at the Ephrata Clothing Center.

**January 21** — Martha wrote that they butchered a beef Tuesday.

**January 24** — Snow piled high on the barnhill. The men had to shovel their way to get supplies.

**February 2** — Sam Zooks had a singing on Sunday p.m. for the benefit of the visitors.

**February 4** — Lizzie made fresh doughnuts all morning. She makes the best.

**February 12** — Eli discouraged by hog prices.

**February 15** — Cousin David A.'s had a get-together for some families who lost their children in accidents. Some came from as far as Indiana.

**February 27** — Abe's crowd was here ice skating. They made hot dogs on the ice.

**March 1** — Eli and Daudy were with a van load of Fisher relatives to Cumberland Co. to help build a hog barn at Joe's.

**March 10** — This morning we had some excitement when I discovered a skunk in the cow barn!

**March 14** — Yesterday was the sale of John F. Yoders. Lizzie and I helped with the chicken corn soup.

**March 18** — Peas are finally in. An extra row this year.

**March 26** — Children flying kites after school in the meadow these days.

**April 4** — Aaron Jr. lost his best work horse. Somehow it must have stumbled down a bank in the cow lane and got under a barb wire fence and couldn't get up.

**April 11** — We took supper with Bishop Junie Stoltzfuses after giving Jonas Fisher a surprise visit in the p.m.

**April 17** — Plowing going good. Neighbor with tractor says it's too wet to get in the fields but our men having no problems.

**April 25** — The boys hauled the grill out of the washhouse and we had grilled sausage for supper. Was a bit nippy to eat outside.

**May 7** — Rachel came to help with planting the flower garden. Her new bread recipe hits the spot!

**May 13** — Fresh asparagus, new rhubarb with tapioca and oranges, and the last of the roosters.

**May 14** — The corn's in! The men worked from dawn till dark for five days. Amos and Elam took turns staying home from school.

**May 29** — School picnic. Lizzie says several families from Honey Brook moving to Missouri. Joe Esh's might be going.

**May 30** — Rain would be appreciated.

**June 1** — I'm trying not to eat too many strawberries. They have too much acid for my arthritis.

**June 14** — We did up 109 quarts of peas. Daudys helped.

**June 20** — Eli and Abe went to the liability meeting at Christ Millers in Mary County, MD.

**June 29** — Weather warm and humid again. Where did spring go? Warm weather is hard on J. J. Miller's Johnny with his condition.

**July 3** — Yesterday afternoon lightning struck close and knocked Jonas A. Smucker down but he got up by himself, and 2 of Jake B's girls were in the cellar and it gave them a hard jolt.

**July 14** — Black raspberries are at an end; sweet corn is on the menu, string beans are plentiful, also weeds in spite of the dry weather.

**July 23** — Wheat is cut and is on shock. Some farmers started to thrash.

**July 30** — The 21 qts. apricots we canned from the neighbor's tree will save us some peach canning.

**August 7** — Clover got washed again today. Has been hard to put up hay at times.

**August 14** — The last two days were spent in painting the school house inside and out, except the stucco. Had a few extra men at the table.

**August 21** — Did up tomato juice today with Lizzie. 56 quarts!

**August 22** — Surprise visit from O'Brien family from New Jersey. Learned to know them last summer at Junie's.

**September 8** — Church services today were held in shed at Sammy Riehls with a large attendance.

**September 16** — Mrs. James B. Hamilton, my roommate when I was in hospital, here for supper tonight. Her husband died in November.

**September 19** — Leaves turning yellow in orchard. First frost last night.

**September 27** — There was a bad accident last evening around 10. A car without lights on the wrong side of the road drove head-on into Levi Kauffman's horse, killing it almost instantly. It threw Levi about 20 feet across the car, breaking his pelvis.

**October 4** — Today a pair of dark frame plastic glasses with bifocals were found along Railroad Ave. in a black case.

**October 12** — John Lapps had a circle letter get-together last week after the meeting.

**October 18** — Eli and the boys working late on the corn. Eli's back tired again.

**October 23** — Helped make snitz pie for church at Aaron Jr's Sunday.

**October 29** — Small game season opened today. What a racket!

**November 1** — On Halloween morn a farm hand came to stay with Aaron Jr's., missing his sister Rebecca's birthday by 39 minutes. He will answer to the name of Jacob, named after Lizzie's father.

**November 3** — Laura Petersheim had a quilting today to give to our teacher (non-Amish).

**November 12** — Today was the wedding at Eli B. Fishers of their oldest daughter Barbara to Samuel E. Zook, son of Pre. Dan Zook. Several hundred ate at dinner, even more for supper.

**November 22** — Another wedding, our sixth this month. Cousin Junie Beiler's Sarah hitched to a Larry Bontrager from Ohio. They met when Sarah went to help her aunt last year.

**December 7** — Little Lydia Smoker is sick with fever and earache so she can't go to school.

**December 17** — Daudy's are going along to the school program. Children working hard on memorization. It tickles me the way Amos is determined.

**December 24** — It's snowing tonight, really coming down. Looks like we'll have a white Christmas.

**December 26** — Second Christmas. Joes came over on the sleigh and Lizzie helped me with the meal. Duck and oyster filling. Cookies galore. A happy time for all.

**December 31** — Another year. "Are we thankful enough the way we have it?"

*As the year goes round so do the seasons. Amish farmers are able to begin plowing earlier in the spring than their tractor-driving neighbors. Because horses are lighter in weight than tractors, they can enter the fields before it is as dry as a tractor requires.*

*Cultivating corn is a precise job but one often given to young children since it does not require exceptional strength.*

*Corn binders cut stalks of corn off at ground level and tie them in bundles. These loads of corn are then chopped and put into silos for the livestock throughout the winter. When the silos are filled, the corn is left to dry. Shell corn is then ground and mixed into short feed for cows.*

# Baskets

Amish Basket quilts come mainly from the Midwest where there was a comparatively more open approach to quiltmaking than among the Pennsylvania Amish. Baskets were popular in general society and the adoption of this pattern by Amish women is somewhat unusual, as Amish quilts tend to avoid the realistic reproduction of an object. There are, however, lovely examples of this design worked by Amish quilters.

Basket patterns use a variety of geometric shapes to create the finished image. Adequate and proper contrasting of fabrics is necessary to enhance the basket design. Where curved handles are a part of the basket, they are appliqued after the Basket block is completed.

The basket, as a design motif, is sometimes quilted on the borders of other quilt patterns. But it is seldom used as the quilting design on a pieced Basket quilt.

On a quilt top the basket blocks are usually alternated with solid blocks of the same size which are quilted with full, flowing lines. Borders provide additional space to display quilting expertise.

*128. Baskets, c. 1910. Cotton, 86 x 66. Ohio. Judi Boisson Antique American Quilts, New York. Several shades of blue are contrasted with the hollow baskets. Tulips are quilted in the alternate plain blocks.*

*Baskets are common containers around Amish farms. Carrying produce from garden to house or from garden to market is often done in baskets.*

*130. Baskets, dated March 21, 1915 and 1945. Cotton, 84 x 61. LaGrange Co., Indiana. Rebecca Haarer. Baskets stand out sharply against a black background.*

**131.** *Baskets, 1920s. Wool, 80 x 80. Lancaster Co., Pennsylvania. Paul and Lorraine Wenrich.*

**132.** *Baskets, c. 1930s. Cotton, 78 x 65. Dover, Delaware. Judi Boisson Antique American Quilts, New York.*

**133.** *Baskets, c. 1915-20. Cotton, wool, 74 x 62. Nappanee, Elkhart Co., Indiana. Norma L. Singleton. Fabric contrast or lack of it varies the appearance of the basket shapes.*

**134.** *Baskets, dated 1908. Cotton, 66 x 84. Montour Co., Pennsylvania. Donna and Jonathan Speigel. A careful blending of subtle colors results in a lovely understated quilt.*

**135.** *Cactus Basket or Star Basket, 1940. Cotton, 75 x 92. Amherst, Wisconsin. Collection of Catherine H. Anthony. Perky baskets appear the same at first glance but study shows subtle differences in the fabrics of the inside petals.*

**136.** *Baskets, c. 1925. Glazed cotton, 92 x 67. Holmes Co., Ohio. Judi Boisson Antique American Quilts, New York. Baskets are pieced and handles appliquéd for this pattern. Note the name embroidered on the inside border.*

# Crazy Quilt

**137.** *Crazy Patch, c. 1900-10. Wool, 80 x 88. Mifflin Co., Pennsylvania. William and Connie Hayes. The interior of this quilt is knotted and borders are quilted.*

An old, old quilt pattern, the Crazy quilt hints of a time when frugality was an inescapable way of life. The Crazy quilt is a collection of scraps and snippets of leftover fabrics or remains of worn-out clothing stitched together with little regard for similarity in shape, size, or color. The result is a wonderful hodgepodge of color and likely a quilt with memories in each patch.

Crazy quilts, although a random collection of shapes and sizes of scraps, are not without an overall plan. The quilt may have a crazy patchwork design over the entire top, or it may be worked in a series of crazy blocks sewn together in a clear-cut pattern, creating order and cohesiveness in the quilt top as a whole.

This is not a time-saving quilt. Any minutes saved by not having to cut patches are soon absorbed in the fancy embroidery work done evenly along the seams of the patches, often in a thread of contrasting color. Occasionally, some fancy embroidery work even appears in the center of one of the larger patches. Perhaps this quilt served as a testing ground for young girls who were learning various embroidery techniques.

Because of the assortment of fabric types and the additional weight of the quilt top (crazy patches are assembled over another piece of fabric) these quilts are often knotted or tied (layers are connected with heavy thread at regular intervals) rather than quilted. Quilting becomes tedious and laborious when going through layers of heavy fabrics.

However, there are outstanding examples of Crazy quilts with superb quilting. Many of these have a crazy patch alternating with a solid patch which is filled with quilting designs. This variety also frequently has wide borders covered with elegant quilting.

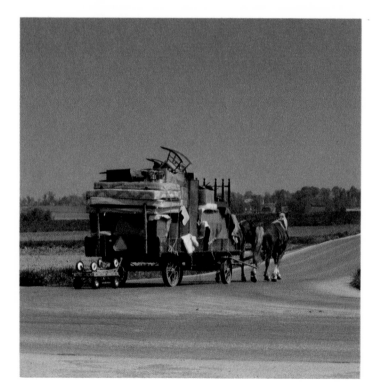

*Moving is a concept common in the history of the Amish. Migrations continue to occur as they look for space and peace from the larger world. The pattern of this moving van is not unlike the composition of the Crazy quilt.*

*139. Crazy Patch, c. 1900. Cotton, wool, 74 x 88. Mifflin Co., Pennsylvania. William B. Wigton. A crazy quilt with a very specific plan, this quilt is modern in its look.*

*140.* Crazy, c. 1915. Wool, 77 x 79. Lancaster Co., Pennsylvania. Privately owned: A beautiful sampling of embroidery stitches outlines each crazy patch. They are set together in an orderly fashion with beautifully quilted plain patches.

*141.* Crazy, c. 1920. Cotton, wool, 79 x 79. Lancaster Co., Pennsylvania. Jay M. and Susen E. Leary. Tiny grapes and grape leaves are quilted on the inside border. Exquisite embroidery decorates the crazy patches.

70

**142.** *Contained Crazy (comforter), c. 1900-10. Wool, cotton flannel, 81 x 67. Arthur, Illinois. Rebecca Haarer.*

**143.** *Scrap Crazy (tied comforter), c. 1925. Denims, cottons, 49 x 71. LaGrange Co., Indiana. Rebecca Haarer. This quilt is made mostly of work pants and shirt materials.*

**144.** *Crazy, c. 1900. Cashmere, cotton, 77 x 72. Berks Co., Pennsylvania. Anna Lois Umble. The maker of this crazy quilt did so with an overall scheme.*

71

# Fan

A bright and cheerful quilt, the Fan is a pattern used largely by Amish women of the Midwest who borrowed it from their neighbors. But its organic quality makes it especially appropriate for these rural farm women. When fans are set in a quilt, all slanting in one direction, they resemble bright flowers leaning toward and drinking in the sunshine. When the blocks are tipped so that the fans stand upright they look like a mass of butterflies in flight. When patches are set opposite each other they remind one of the agitation of a butterchurn and when all four points are assembled together the fans form a wheel.

The Fan quilt may be a combination of piecing and appliquéing or it may be completely pieced. When the former method is used, the fans are first pieced, then appliquéd onto a background square. This means of construction is especially prevalent when the edge of the fan is scalloped.

Embroidery around the edges of the fans is an additional feature on some Amish Fan quilts. Quilting surrounds the fan design and decorates the borders.

*145. Fan, 1904. 79 x 80, Berks Co., Pennsylvania. Anna Lois Umble. One patch was done without the addition of embroidery around the fan.*

*New growth coming from the old is a universal theme. It is also found in the Amish community, both in nature and the church. The Fan pattern is reflected in the reel of this binder as it sheaves the wheat.*

*147. Fan, dated 1927. Cotton, sateen, 76 x 85. Elkhart Co., Indiana. Diana Leone. Several pieces of black velvet add richness to this vibrant quilt.*

**148.** *Fan, dated 1904. Cotton, wool, 74 x 63. Topeka, LaGrange Co., Indiana. Rebecca Haarer. Light colored fans look feathery soft against their dark background.*

**149.** *Fan, dated 1943. Cotton, wool, 81 x 81. Lancaster Co., Pennsylvania. Jay M. and Susen E. Leary. Quilted roses fill the border and spaces above the fans.*

74

**150.** *Fan, dated 1913. Cotton, wool, 64 x 76. Shipshewana, LaGrange Co., Indiana. Rebecca Haarer. The date is prominently displayed in the center of this quilt. Note the different treatment of corners on the inside border.*

**151.** *Fan, c. 1900. Wool, 83 x 70. Mifflin Co., Pennsylvania. Judi Boisson Antique American Quilts, New York. Bright yellow and blue fans occupy the corners with assorted colors in the center.*

**152.** *Circular Fans, 1890s. Worsted wool, 76 x 78. Holmes Co., Ohio. Judi Boisson Antique American Quilts, New York.*

# Ocean Waves

Ocean Waves is a pattern frequently seen in Midwestern Amish quilts but rarely used by the Pennsylvania Amish. The pattern exemplifies its name with small triangles creating movement and currents in the lines of the quilt.

Because of their limited travel and the landlocked locations of Amish settlements, the makers of these quilts likely never saw ocean waves. Despite that, the many variations of this pattern capture the mix of quiet and storm that bespeaks the ocean.

In general, Midwestern Amish quilters used brighter colors and more diverse patterns but paid less attention to the details of quilting than did Pennsylvania Amish quilters. In Ocean Waves the colors are generally quite bright. Yellow, a frequent choice for this pattern, appears less frequently among Pennsylvania Amish quilts but is common in the Midwest. As is typical of many Midwestern quilts, the borders and bindings of Ocean Waves are often narrower than on Pennsylvania quilts. Furthermore, instead of the elaborate feathered quilting often found on Pennsylvania borders, Midwestern quilting is often the more simple and easily executed cable design.

*153. Ocean Waves, dated August 20, 1919. Cotton, 72 x 84. Holmes Co., Ohio. Judi Boisson Antique American Quilts, New York. The gray background seems to perk up the colors in the interior of the quilt.*

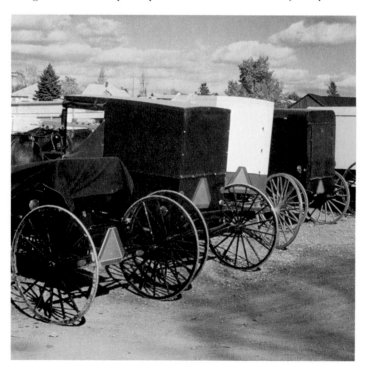

*The orange, slow-moving-vehicle symbols on the rear of these buggies look like the triangles on an Ocean Waves quilt. This hitching post has attracted a diversity of Amish buggies.*

*155. Ocean Waves, c. 1930. Cotton, 89 x 74. Holmes Co., Ohio. Judi Boisson Antique American Quilts, New York.*

**156.** *Ocean Waves, c. 1930-40. Cotton, 76 x 69. Holmes Co., Ohio. Judi Boisson Antique American Quilts, New York. Touches of bright yellow and several other light fabrics add spark to this quilt. A narrow inner border frames the pieced design.*

**157.** *Ocean Waves, c. 1940s. Cotton, 71 x 78. Holmes Co., Ohio. Judi Boisson Antique American Quilts, New York. The blue-green background on this quilt seems especially appropriate for the Ocean Waves pattern.*

**158.** Ocean Waves, dated February 10, 1934. Cotton, 80 x 92. Elkhart Co., Indiana. Rebecca Haarer. A pattern typical of Midwestern Amish, this quilt shows the use of yellow and lavender not frequently used by Amish in eastern Pennsylvania.

**159.** Ocean Waves Variation — "Zig-zag Diamond," c. 1910. Cotton, 70 x 78. Holmes Co., Ohio. Judi Boisson Antique American Quilts, New York.

# Roman Stripe

Roman Stripe is a pattern used mainly by Midwestern Amish quilters. A quilt of very simple construction, it may also be referred to as Shadows. In it, square blocks are equally divided with one half being a solid fabric and the other half being a series of diagonal strips ending with a triangle. The strips of brightly colored fabric are usually arranged in a random fashion. Although simply constructed, the overall effect of this pattern is an almost shocking burst of color and energy.

The arrangement of the quilt blocks can totally change the impact of the top. Blocks may be set in the quilt with each triangle pointing in the same direction. Another arrangement with the blocks put together in a zig-zag fashion creates the image of jagged streaks of lightning. And if the blocks are placed with four triangles coming together a diamond is formed. Many other possibilities exist and have been tried by the creative quilter.

*160. Roman Stripe, dated 1934. Wool (small piece of velvet in center), 82 x 84. Topeka, LaGrange Co., Indiana. Rebecca Haarer. Use of a brown background makes this a quilt with a feeling of warmth, made by Susie Miller for her daughter as a wedding gift.*

*Sharp and easy angles of farm architecture could well be the inspiration for some quilt patterns. Parallel and alternating diagonal lines reflect both quilt lines and barn lines.*

**162.** *Roman Stripe, dated 1906. Wool, 81 x 62. Holmes Co., Ohio. The Darwin D. Bearley Collection.*

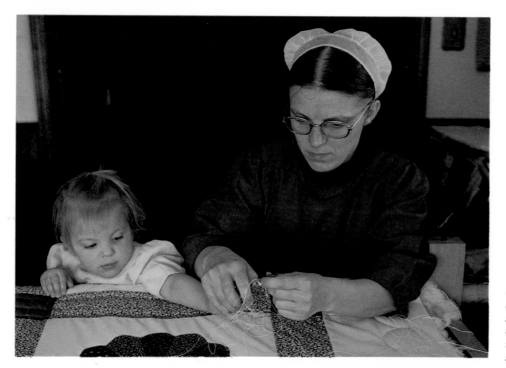

# A Quilting

For a people who choose to do without radio, TV, movies, and many types of entertainment enjoyed by the larger society, visiting is vital. Visiting happens regularly and spontaneously. Unannounced guests are always welcome. Even if a visit happens to be near mealtime, the company is heartily invited to stay and eat. Families often spend Sunday afternoons or evenings with relatives or friends. It is the slower pace of the Amish lifestyle that allows time for the simple pleasures of human interaction. Gathered friends may play games together or, more likely, talk about events in each other's lives.

## Quiltings Mix Work and Visiting

A quilting is an all-day occasion to do some fun "work"—and visit. It is generally hosted by a woman who has one or more quilts to quilt. She may choose to make it a "sisters day" whereupon she invites all her sisters, or she may issue a broader invitation to specific friends and neighbors. Quiltings take place throughout the year but they are more frequent during less busy seasons on the farm.

Usually quilting begins early in the morning after mothers have given their school-age children a proper breakfast and seen them off for the day. Pre-school children attend quiltings, and since there are usually a group of them, have as much fun playing as their mothers have quilting. Older children may be asked to keep a supply of threaded needles on hand and they help to watch their younger siblings. The quilt, stretched tightly in a quilting frame, provides a wonderful imaginary house for these youngsters.

## "Putting In" the Quilt

The first job to be done (if the hostess has not already completed it) is "putting in" the quilt. That involves stretching the back, lining, and top of the quilt tautly in the frame. The most common type of frame allows quilters to work on all four sides of the quilt at the same time. It is a simple structure with four strips of wood held together by C-clamps. The top and bottom ends of the quilt back are pinned or basted to a strip of heavy fabric which has been tacked along the edge of two of the frame's wooden strips. The back is then tightly stretched between these two strips and the remaining two wooden strips are laid along the sides of the quilt back. The pieces of wood are clamped at the corners, thus making the quilt back a tight, flat surface. The frame, now stretched to its proper size, is then laid across the backs of four chairs making it an appropriate height for quilting. Next, the lining is laid on the quilt back and pinned securely on all sides. And finally the top, with its tracings for quilting designs, is stretched over the back and lining and pinned tightly in place. The bedcover is ready to be quilted.

## A Quilting Pecking Order

A typical quilting will involve anywhere from six to twelve women. Seating positions around the quilting frame are often good-naturedly negotiated since no one wants to sit next to and be outshone by the best or fastest quilter! And less experienced quilters choose to sit where there are straight lines to quilt since they are more easily managed than curved lines.

*This detail shows five typical quilting designs: 1) pumpkin seed, 2) cross hatch, 3) cable, 4) fan, and 5) feather.*

*Quilting templates are often made from scrap pieces of cardboard. After the design is cut away, the pattern is traced on the quilt top and then covered with tiny stitches.*

The women, sitting around all four sides of the frame, begin quilting at the outer edge and work toward the center as far as they are able to reach. When all the women along the top and bottom of the frame have quilted to their maximum stretch, the quilt is ready to "roll." The clamps at the four corners of the frame are released and the finished sections of the quilt are gently rolled onto the wood until the unquilted surface is brought to the edge. "Rolling" can take place only from the two ends of the frame. Therefore, when the quilters along the side reach their maximum they must either find and squeeze into a new position at the ends, begin another quilt in another frame, or find something else to do. Those who choose the latter frequently help the hostess prepare lunch.

# Eating Belongs with a Quilting

The noon meal is compensation for the time and effort supplied by the invited quilters. It is a highlight of the day. The hostess prepares a full-course meal and serves it with pride. Kitchen helpers may be women who were invited to the quilting but would rather not quilt. For them, being in the kitchen is as enjoyable as being around the frame. However, if a woman is assigned to kitchen duty when she would rather quilt, it can be humbling. This sometimes happens to teenaged girls whose stitches are not yet tiny or neat enough to meet the hostess' quilting standards. It is an honor for young girls to be invited to quilt at a quilting. Quilting resumes again after lunch. Women are free to come and go as they are able. Some stay the whole day. Others come for only a few hours.

# A Strengthening Time

A quilting is more than a work day. It is an occasion to share household tips, garden hints, home remedies, child-rearing information, and the latest news about marriages, births, and deaths. Such a gathering of women with common backgrounds, interests, and goals provides a chance for them to talk at length about their daily lives. A quilting reminds these women of the support they have and gives them a break from daily routine. For hard-working farm women, such an event can be a refreshing one-day vacation.

# Quilting for Others

Quiltings are not only held in private homes. The Amish, though separate from the larger world, are not unaware of global needs. Amish women readily participate in quiltings held by the Mennonite Central Committee, a world-wide relief organization that sends food, clothing, and personnel all over the world. Amish women also lend their skills to community projects. Many volunteer fire companies hold quiltings several times a year to produce quilts to sell at their benefit auctions. Since the Amish rely on the services of their local fire companies, they support them actively as volunteer firefighters and contribute time and energy to their quiltings and benefit suppers.

When a quilting day is ended and the quilt completed, it stands as a tangible symbol of group effort. It portrays not only the skill of these women, but also the strong supportive love that envelopes this community and keeps it vibrant and alive despite the pressures of the modern world.

# Tumbling Blocks

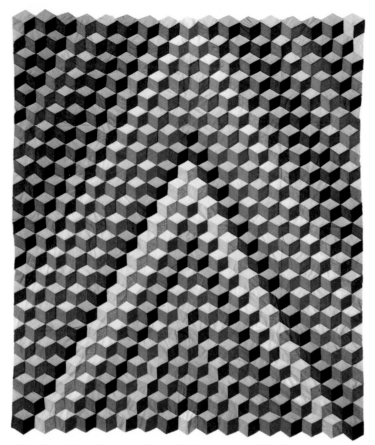

The Tumbling Blocks or Baby Blocks is a simple quilt but one with an intriguing interplay of color and apparent dimension. One can gaze at the Tumbling Block quilt for some time before all of its patterns emerge. By using a single diamond shape and the varied placement of colors, a quiltmaker can create an optical illusion of cubes, hexagons, stars, and diamonds. Occasionally the arrangement of colors also produces a large overall design on the quilt surface.

To achieve the illusion of stacked cubes one must have at least three fabrics in varying intensities of color—one dark, one medium, and one light. The diamonds must be arranged in a hexagon formation with the dark, medium, and light fabrics being used in the same positions throughout the quilt. If diamonds are simply arranged in a random fashion a star is likely to be the dominant emerging pattern.

Quilting stitches generally follow the outline of the diamonds on the pieced top. Surrounding borders are quilted in more fanciful designs.

*166. Tumbling Blocks — Pyramid Variation, c. 1930-40. Cotton, rayon (worsted wool-cotton blend), 85 x 99. Ohio. Judi Boisson Antique American Quilts, New York. This is only a quilt top but shows a very successful achievement of a design within a pattern.*

*Families work together in all aspects of farm life. Here father and sons work beside each other loading straw, an image similar to Tumbling Blocks.*

*168. Tumbling Blocks, c. 1930. Cotton, 74 x 67. Ohio. Judi Boisson Antique American Quilts, New York. Well organized stacks of cubes form the body of this magnificent quilt.*

*169. Tumbling Blocks, c. 1940s. Cotton, 83 x 76. Kokomo, Indiana. Rebecca Haarer.*

*170. Tumbling Blocks, c. 1925. Cotton, 70 x 79. Holmes Co., Ohio. Judi Boisson Antique American Quilts, New York. Dark, rich colors give this quilt depth. Note the combination of clamshell and diamond motifs quilted on the border.*

171. *Tumbling Blocks (Baby Blocks), c. 1925. Cotton, 80 x 74. Geauga Co., Ohio. The Darwin D. Bearley Collection. Effective use of three colors (plus the binding) make this a successful illusion.*

172. *Tumbling Blocks (Baby Blocks), c. 1930. Cotton, 80 x 98. LaGrange Co., Indiana. Collection of Catherine H. Anthony. Red in combination with two shades of blue give the illusion of stacked cubes.*

173. *Tumbling Blocks, dated November 2, 1929. Cotton, 71 x 75. LaGrange Co., Indiana. Rebecca Haarer.*

# Bow Tie

It is fascinating to observe that a group who chooses to avoid the wearing of men's ties makes the Bow Tie quilt pattern with such flair. Obviously there is much creative freedom permitted in quiltmaking. Although considered unnecessary and attention-getting as a clothing accessory, the bow tie as a design is not viewed as wrong if it is used within clear boundaries.

This is a delightful pattern with sprightly little bow ties nearly dancing across the quilt surface. Most often they are arranged in diagonal, vertical, or horizontal rows. On occasion they are set at angles to form a circle on the quilt top.

Possibly an alteration of the basic Four-Patch, the Bow Tie is much more difficult to construct because of the tiny square in the center of the tie. This requires that the four surrounding squares have one corner trimmed diagonally. When piecing, this angled corner must be set in against the bow tie, a task not easily achieved by beginners.

Quilting generally outlines the ties and becomes more plentiful on the one or more borders framing them.

*174. Bow Tie Variation, c. 1900. Cotton, wool, 66 x 82. Loudenville, Ohio. Judi Boisson Antique American Quilts, New York. Bow ties are not as easily seen in this arrangement of the pattern.*

*Dress regulations within the various Amish groups are generally quite severe. Black outerwear is common. Black felt hats are worn by the men and boys in cold weather, straw hats in hot. Bow ties are only worn by Amish quilts, not Amish males.*

*176. Bow Tie, dated 1919. Cotton, 70 x 84. Nappanee, Elkhart Co., Indiana. Rebecca Haarer. Set in straight horizontal rows, the ties seem to be arranged for some performance.*

*177. Bow Tie, c. late 1940s. Cotton, 75 x 68. Holmes Co., Ohio. Nancy Meng. Tiny four-patches form the corners of the inner border. One bow tie in the corner is facing the opposite directon.*

*178. Bow Tie, c. 1930. Cotton, 78 x 71. Elkhart Co., Indiana. Joseph M. B. Sarah. Trailing tulips fill the inner border on this well-organized quilt. Shades of black vary in some patches.*

*179. Bow Tie, c. 1910-20. Cotton, 68 x 84. Collected LaGrange Co., Indiana. Rebecca Haarer. Quilted hearts filled with a floral design cover the border of this two-color quilt.*

# Robbing Peter to Pay Paul

This pattern, known to quilters in general, was likely borrowed by an Amish woman from a non-Amish quilter friend. The quilt is often done in only two colors which enhances the power of the finished design.

Robbing Peter to Pay Paul is a logical label for this design: a section of one patch is robbed to fill a gap in the next. The positive and negative aspect of this pattern creates a sharp, clear circular design on the quilt top.

Curved lines make this a pattern for a quilter with experience since a pieced pattern with curved lines increases the potential for puckers and buckles. Curved edges must be very accurately cut and sewn to achieve a smooth, flat finish.

Quilting designs are stitched on the borders and in the larger patch between circles. Other pieced sections are simply outlined with quilting.

*180. Robbing Peter to Pay Paul, 1905-10. Cotton, 68 x 74. Nappanee, Elkhart Co., Indiana. Rebecca Haarer. Light and dark fabrics provide excellent contrast for this pattern of positive and negative space.*

*181. Robbing Peter to Pay Paul, c. 1910-15. Cotton, 82 x 66. LaGrange Co., Indiana. Joseph M. B. Sarah. The smooth lines of this curved pattern must have been crafted by a master quiltmaker.*

# Monkey Wrench

**182.** *Monkey Wrench, c. 1924. Cotton, 83 x 69. Elkhart Co., Indiana. Rebecca Haarer.*

Another name for the Monkey Wrench design is Hole in the Barn Door. Both are apt descriptions for the pattern created by this combination of geometric shapes.

There are not sharp lines drawn between domestic tasks and farm tasks in an Amish home. Women are generally aware of and part of decisions made concerning the farm operations. Nor is it unusual to see women helping in the fields, milking cows, and tending chickens.

Perhaps this quilt pattern is a statement of the overlap in domestic chores, farm work, and the often more pleasurable task of quiltmaking. The monkey wrench (pipe wrench) is a tool found on any farm. One never knows when an implement will need minor repairs during planting or harvest season. And perhaps the Hole in the Barn Door label was inspired by an imaginative woman who saw the possibility of a quilt pattern in the cut-out of the stable door, designed to provide ventilation for farm animals.

The design is achieved through use of triangles and squares or rectangles to form a square patch. These patches may be set straight or tipped on an angle in the quilt top. When set on an angle, the blocks are set alternately with solid squares of fabric which lend themselves well to a fancy quilting design. The blocks are usually framed by one or more borders filled with flowing quilting.

*The Monkey Wrench quilt is also called Hole in the Barn Door. Is there any question about why?!*

*184. Monkey Wrench, 1911. Cotton, 82 x 72. LaGrange Co., Indiana. Rebecca Haarer. Blocks have been pieced and arranged in symmentry throughout this quilt.*

**185.** *Hole in the Barn Door, c. 1915-20. Cotton, 82 x 69. Ohio. The Darwin D. Bearley Collection. Beautiful quilting fills in alternate patches of this pieced design.*

**186.** *Hole in the Barn Door Variation, c. 1910. Wool, 72 x 84. Arthur, Illinois. Rebecca Haarer. Likely a scrap quilt, this one uses a myriad of colors throughout.*

**187.** *Combination Eight Point Star-Hole in the Barn Door, dated January 27, 1942. Cotton, 88 x 76. Emma, LaGrange Co., Indiana. Rebecca Haarer. This quilter successfully combined two patterns into one. It was made by Mrs. Menno Yoder who made several such quilts — one for each of her seven children.*

94

# Carolina Lily

**188.** *North Carolina Lily, c. 1920-30. Cotton, 75 x 77. Holmes Co., Ohio. The Darwin D. Bearley Collection. Pattern, colors, borders, binding, and quilting make this a real showpiece.*

**189.** *Carolina Lily, 1883-93. Cotton, 76 x 76. Davidsville, Somerset Co., Pennsylvania. Romaine S. Sala. The papers hand-stitched on the corners of this quilt read as follows: "Romaine's quilt pieced and quilted by G Pa Kaufmans Mother Christian Johns Kaufman" and "This is Nora's quilt."*

It is rare to find the Carolina Lily pattern among Amish quilts. And yet, its occasional presence indicates that a few Amish women were captivated by its beauty and did create quilts of this design.

The Amish have a high respect for nature and its gifts. Living close to the soil makes them more conscious of the earth's bounty and beauty. But because the Amish take seriously the Old Testament commandment against making graven images, they have traditionally kept from reproducing realistic images from nature. But, as in all of life, there are exceptions. And so occasionally, the Carolina Lily image appears.

The lilies and baskets of this pattern are pieced triangles, squares, and rectangles. Stems and handles are appliqued, a technique seldom used in antique Amish quilts.

This is a showy pattern and if a quiltmaker went to the trouble of piecing it, she was likely to cover it with extravagant quilting designs. There is ample space between flower baskets and on borders to absorb this exuberant work.

# Shoo-fly

**190.** *Shoo-fly Variation, dated January 9, 1913. Cotton, 72 x 84. LaGrange Co., Indiana. Rebecca Haarer.*

A visitor to an Amish home need not be there long to discover the outstanding culinary skills of these plain people. Their food is basic, plentiful and, for the most part, home-grown. Since the Amish remain largely an agrarian, hard-working people, foods tend to be heavier and richer than many more sedentary urban- and suburbanites can handle. Cream, butter, eggs, meat, vegetables, and even fruit are readily accessible on many farms. They are therefore used in cooking, creating a delightful spread on the farm kitchen table.

One of the well-known pies associated with the Amish is shoo-fly pie. It is a sweet rich dessert with a gooey molasses bottom topped with spicy cake and baked in a flaky pie crust. Because the pie is so sweet it is said to have attracted flies during the baking process. Hence the name shoo-fly.

Since the Amish are well-known for both delights it seems appropriate that a quilt should bear the name of this notorious dessert, although no visual connection is apparent. The block is a basic nine-patch with some of the blocks halved to create triangles. The same pattern is also known as a Fence Row by some quilters. Patches are generally framed with one or more borders providing plenty of space for the skilled quilter.

**191.** *Shoo-fly, c. 1925. Wool, cotton sateen, 68 x 72. Mifflin Co., Pennsylvania. William B. Wigton. Quilted cloverleafs fill alternate plain patches and hearts cover the inner border on this bedcover.*

*192. Fence Row, 1908. Cotton, 84 x 72. Nappanee, Elkhart Co., Indiana. Rebecca Haarer. Background fabric is pieced and varies slightly in shade but it only seems to add to the overall beauty of the quilt.*

# Bear Paw

The inspiration for the Bear Paw pattern is said to have come from frontier days when bear tracks were commonly found in the snow or mud of wooded farmland. An encounter with wildlife was a daily possibility and was captured in this quilt design. The pattern was borrowed by the Amish community and used largely by Midwestern Amish quilters. A slight variation of the pattern is also known as Cross and Crown. This name carries the religious significance of Jesus' death on the cross and the crown of thorns that he wore.

The pattern looks complex because of its jagged edges but the shapes make construction quite simple. Triangles forming the bear's toes are sewn together to form squares. The squares are connected to a larger square and rectangles form the connecting cross pieces.

This design's most realistic look is achieved when strongly contrasting colors are used making the paw stand out sharply against the background. Quilting generally outlines the paw shape and decorates alternate squares as well as the borders.

*193. Cross and Crown, c. 1925. Cotton, 87 x 64. Elkhart Co., Indiana. Rebecca Haarer. This variation of the Bear Paw design places the outer triangles in an alternate direction.*

*194. Bear Paw, dated 1939. Cotton, 85 x 71. Ohio. Judi Boisson Antique American Quilts, New York. The sawtooth inner border ties in nicely with the jagged Bear Paw design.*

*196. Bear Paw, dated 1893. Cotton, 85 x 69. Loudenville, Ohio. Judi Boisson Antique American Quilts, New York. Quilting designs are not elaborate but are very extensive and excellently crafted. The red inner border and binding give life to this quilt.*

*195. Bear Paw, c. 1915. Cotton, 72 x 64. La-Grange Co., Indiana. Joseph M. B. Sarah.*

# Crown of Thorns

197. *Crown of Thorns, c. 1920. Cotton, 76 x 88. Collected LaGrange Co., Indiana. Rebecca Haarer.*

*Some quilt patterns are possibly taken from biblical themes. This single row of corn stalks also reminds one of the Crown of Thorns motif.*

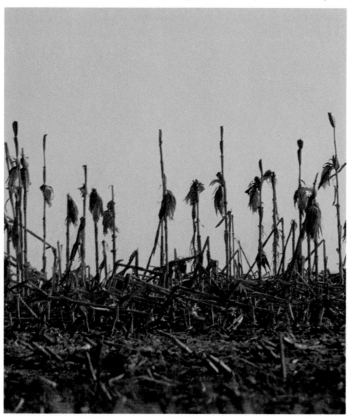

The Amish are a people deeply committed to God. However, most of these groups are not openly expressive about their faith. In general, Old Order groups do not proselytize. The groups are growing in number mostly because of their large families. It is significant that a high percentage of young people choose to join and remain in the Amish church.

Crown of Thorns is one of the few Amish quilts with distinctively religious connections. It directs one's thinking to the Passion and suffering of Christ. The Amish commitment of discipleship even to death remains strong. Theirs is a spirit of humility and awe before God the Creator and a willingness to give up "worldly" distractions so as to follow the teachings of Jesus more closely. The Amish are at peace with their convictions but do not look down on outsiders whose understandings lead to a different way of life.

The Crown of Thorns pattern is a series of triangles and squares making construction simple. However, the visual impact of the quilt is much more complex. Ornate quilting is reserved for non-pieced blocks and borders.

***199.*** *Crown of Thorns, c. 1930. Cotton sateen, 80 x 94. Holmes Co., Ohio. Collection of Catherine H. Anthony.*

# Pinwheel

**200.** *Pinwheel Variation, dated February 12, 1925. Cotton, 76 x 66. LaGrange Co., Indiana. Rebecca Haarer. This variation is also called Twin Sisters.*

**201.** *Crazy Ann, dated March 1915. Cotton, 86 x 78. Topeka, LaGrange Co., Indiana. Rebecca Haarer. This Pinwheel variation has initials embroidered in the bottom right corner.*

The windmill turns effortlessly in the breeze creating power to pump water to Amish houses and barns. The Amish have drawn fine but distinct lines on energy use.

They do not see electricity itself as wrong, but they do believe that purchasing it from local power companies links them physically to the larger world. Furthermore, such easy availability of electricity would present them with temptations that could undermine their family and community life—radio and television, for example, are seen as threatening.

By choosing to live without electricity, the Amish have become inventive in finding alternatives. They use gas, diesel, and pneumatic power to operate their refrigerators, kitchen appliances, and power tools. They live without electric lights, perhaps the greatest inconvenience modern Americans would feel in an Amish home. Instead, the Amish use gas lamps which provide bright and adequate light, but must be pumped, lit, and carried from room to room in the house. That choice in itself keeps a family physically together, evening after evening.

The Pinwheel quilt looks like the spinning blades of a windmill and is a gentle reminder of this less hurried and separate way of life. Although the pattern is used by many quiltmakers it seems to have a special link to the Amish. Triangles and rectangles form the pattern of blades and correct usage of color gives the illusion of movement. Pieced blocks are often alternated with solid blocks which encourage an energetic quilting caper. Borders are also clean open spaces waiting for the skilled artistry of the quilter.

**202.** *Pinwheel, dated 1929. Wool, 76½ x 67½. Elkhart Co., Indiana. Donna and Jonathan Speigel. Tulip designs are quilted on the plain patches between the pieced blocks.*

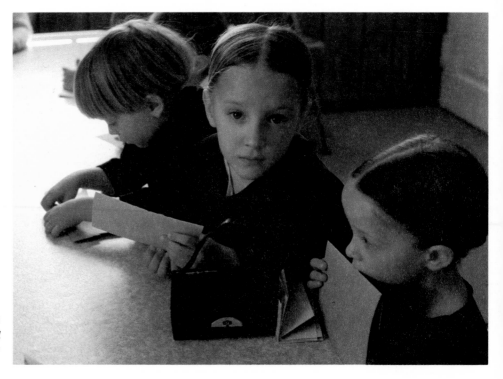

*Children are considered a gift from God by the Amish. They learn the joy, obedience and difficulty of the Amish way from the time they are born.*

# Contentment within Limitations

Being *in* the world but not *of* the world is a concept understood and practiced by the Amish in a radical way. This separateness is evidenced in their mode of dress, different language and independent school systems. They maintain these lines through a strong community and personal accountability to the brotherhood.

Most North Americans find their sense of personal worth in their job and its accomplishments. They thrive on a strong spirit of competition. But in the Amish world, values are different. Personal fulfillment is found within the group. Individualism is not erased but it is tempered by the goals and purposes of the community of faith. The good of the community is placed above one's personal gain. Being at peace with limitations is crucial to being Amish. Yet it seems that it is these very disciplines that inspire their creativity. Witness the ways the Amish have invented to maintain their lines of separateness without causing paralyzing hardships for themselves.

## Living Without Electricity

Most Amish do not use electrical power from their local utility works. But that does not mean they are without energy. Many Amish are dairy farmers who must keep their milk cool while it waits to be picked up by a tank truck. So most use diesel driven refrigeration units, thus bypassing the need for electricity from high tension lines.

Increasingly more and more equipment is being attached to these diesel motors. In some communities it is common to rig up an air compressor to the motor. Air lines are run to the barn, shop, house and well. Adapters have been designed by Amish craftsmen to permit drills, lathes and many other kinds of hand and stationary equipment to be pneumatically powered. An air line to the bottom of the farm well supplies water to the house and barn. And in the house, mixers, blenders and washing machines may be energized by the same air compressor connected to the diesel motor that cools the bulk milk tank.

On farms without air compressors, water may be pumped by a windmill to a reservoir. This reservoir is often an up-ended tank train car placed at the top of the barnhill or some other point of high elevation. Simple gravity then supplies water to the barn and household.

Again, any generalization overlooks exceptions. Some Amish do use their local electrical company, others continue to reject the use of diesel motors for cooling milk.

## Strong Lines Create Energy Within

Many outsiders find these inventions to be grossly inconsistent. But to understand these people one must not forget the Amish community's intent—to draw clearly defined lines that provide solidarity for the group and separation from the world.

Belonging to a group with well-defined rules could seem stifling. And yet when perimeters are outlined, members find freedom to move around within them. When they agree with and understand the guidelines, they tap their own ingenuity to find resourceful ways to be content. The Amish farmer does not envy his non-Amish neighbor who plows with a tractor. He knows a tractor is not an option. He sets his mind to enjoy farming the Amish way. His responsibility is to be a good steward of God's earth. And his perception of how to accomplish that task has been formed within the context of a group who supports and shares his values.

*On Amish farms, young and old, male and female help with field and garden work. It is common to see women in command of a team of horses and mules in the field.*

## Finding Beauty in the Simple

The Amish have developed a character of contentment. They enjoy the basics of life without thinking about the ruffles. For example, their food is usually prepared in standard, sturdy ways. They haven't nurtured a romance with fancy cuisine. Instead, robust food in plentiful quantity is the rule.

Nor is decorating a major concern of Amish women. This does not mean they have no aesthetic appreciation. Amish homes frequently contain beautifully handpainted chairs and chests. Most women own a set of decorated china and pieces of it are often displayed on a buffet or server when it is not in use. Handpainted mottos hang on bare walls. And in general, homes are meticulously clean and tidy.

Even in the clothing that Amish women make for themselves and their families, although it follows a prescribed pattern, there is evident a sense of pride in doing it well.

Children, who grow up without television and few mass-produced, store-bought toys, learn early to have fun instead with their imagination and many brothers and sisters. A farm—and animals—offer many possibilities for play.

The Amish world is not perfect. For instance, Amish families struggle with relationships and economic tensions like their non-Amish neighbors. But the Amish do not need to face their problems in isolation. They have each other for strength and understanding.

*The Amish caution on modern technology has resulted in their own collection of inventions. Here is a hydraulic plow, complete with padded seat, which remains within the church regulations that stipulate steel wheels.*

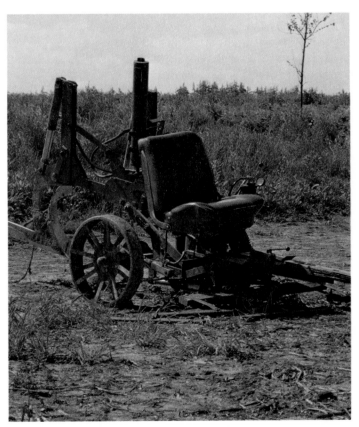

# Friendship or Album Quilt

**206.** *Detail of Plate 208 on facing page.*

*There is security and joy in belonging to a people. The community gathers at important times: at barnraisings and quiltings, at weddings, funerals and other special occasions. Here people are getting ready to go home after a Sunday morning worship service.*

There are few gifts more gratefully received than a Friendship quilt. It consists of quilt patches (sometimes simple square patches, sometimes pieced designs or shaped patches) that are distributed to friends of the recipient. Usually the planning of the quilt is done by one person who decides the number and size of the patches to make an adequate quilt. Each patch is signed by its maker in embroidery stitching. In fact, frequently the patches are filled with embroidered designs, especially if the block is a plain square. Finished blocks are then assembled and quilted, often at a quilting where many of the patchmakers are present. The finished quilt is then given to their mutual friend.

The occasion for the making of a Friendship quilt may be monumental or quite incidental. Sometimes they are made by parents and/or students for a terminating school teacher. Frequently a young Amish girl about to be married will hand out patches to her friends to embroider and sign. She will then host a quilting to finish the quilt in celebration of her coming marriage.

The two square-patch Friendship quilts shown here were made by the community of two sisters following the death of their mother when the girls were quite young. This gesture was a tangible sign of caring and support by the surrounding families.

The third quilt shown here in the Spools design is made of a series of patches gathered over a period of two years by an Amish woman. She sent paper templates to Amish friends in other communities and asked them to cut a patch, sign it, and return it to her. The result was a unique collection of colors and fabrics which she then pieced and quilted. What a lovely remembrance of friends far away! The quilt includes patches from Indiana, Illinois, Ohio, Wisconsin, and Pennsylvania.

**208.** *Friendship, pieced 1933-34, quilted 1937. Cotton, 85 x 68. Nappanee, Elkhart Co., Indiana. Susan Wickey. A collection of patches from several states, this quilt represents long distance friendships. The patches were collected over a two-year period by Susan Mast. She pieced the quilt and then had a quilting for neighborhood friends.*

**209.** *Friendship, dated 1939. Cotton, 74 x 87. Nappanee, Elkhart Co., Indiana. Mrs. Mary Bontrager.*

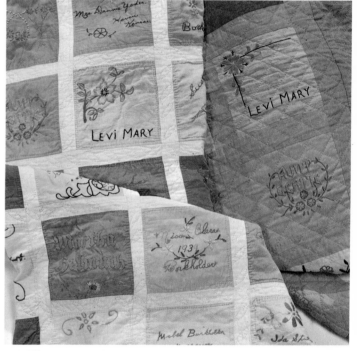

**210.** *These two patches, made by the same woman, can be found on the two quilts pictured at left. The quilts were made for two young sisters after the death of their mother.*

**211.** *Friendship, dated 1939. Cotton, 74 x 87. Nappanee, Elkhart Co., Indiana. Rebecca Haarer.*

# Rail Fence

The Rail Fence uses only one basic shape in its construction—the rectangle. Patches are stitched together to form a square and are then pieced at alternating right angles to each other. It is an unusually simple quilt but with the careful use of color, intriguing patterns emerge on the finished quilt top.

Quilting lines are generally simple. Pieced patches are usually outlined or quilted in straight lines with more elaborate stitching used on the border(s).

The Rail Fence is not unique to Amish quilters. It is easy to imagine, however, that women on farms with their maze of fences would be attracted to this pattern.

Perhaps the simple beauty of the Rail Fence quilt hints at the simplicity of living within clear, well-defined boundaries.

*212. Rail Fence, c. 1930. Cotton, 84 x 76. Loudenville, Ohio. Judi Boisson Antique American Quilts, New York. Because of its visual images this pattern is sometimes known as "Streak of Lightning."*

*213. Rail Fence, c. 1920. Cotton, 80 x 68. LaGrange Co., Indiana. Joseph M. B. Sarah.*

# Garden Maze

Garden Maze describes a pattern of square fabric blocks, each surrounded by elaborate sashing. The two narrow borders that outline each square connect neighboring squares and intersect between their corners. Although the inside square could be left empty, it is commonly filled with a pieced design. The pieced design and the surrounding maze are usually contained within a quilted border.

The Garden Maze quilt is as neat and orderly as an Amish garden. Few gardeners surpass the meticulous care given by Amish growers. Rows are straight and neat. Flowers often surround the garden edge giving it a burst of bright color. Weeds are nipped in the bud and plants are carefully tended. For many women, spring fever and garden fever come hand in hand and they eagerly await the chance to work in the soil.

Although gardening is thoroughly enjoyed by many Amish families, it is not just a hobby. Preservation of food occupies a large part of the women's energies throughout the summer and by the onset of winter their larders are full of canned, pickled, and preserved vegetables, relishes, jams, fruits, and meats.

Quilting takes a back seat to these seasonal requirements. But in the fall and winter when days are spent indoors, quilting resumes at full force. It is a happy balance when the necessary work of life is so wholeheartedly enjoyed and incorporated into their more relaxed tasks. The Amish seem to have mastered this art in many areas.

*214. Rolling Stone in Garden Maze, c. 1910-20. Cotton, 67 x 78. Collected Elkhart Co., Indiana. Harry Brorby.*

*Men help most in preparation of the soil for the family garden. Here two sons help ready the garden for planting while the team rests in the shade, waiting for another stint in the fields.*

**216.** *Cups and Saucers in Garden Maze, c. 1919. Cotton, wool, 83 x 68. LaGrange Co., Indiana. Rebecca Haarer. The Garden Maze is the sash work surrounding the smaller pieced designs.*

# Railroad Crossing

The Railroad Crossing pattern, when used by Amish quilters, is found mainly among Midwestern Amish. This pattern varies extensively. The "crossings" become the main focus when a series of narrow horizontal strips resembling railroad ties are assembled. In other variations the main emphasis is on the space between the "crossings" which is broken into a collage of brightly colored triangles. The entire pieced top is framed with one or more borders.

Although most travel by the Amish is limited to horse-drawn carriages, they are permitted to use public transportation. Many Amish take advantage of local bus routes and for extended travel will use trains.

It is also common for them to hire a van and driver for a fee who then serve much like a taxi with the family or families having direct control of its route. This allows them to make stops for visiting or shopping enroute to their destination. In areas with high concentrations of Amish there are usually several persons who offer van service. For short trips to town or to a doctor where use of the carriage is not practical it is not unusual for the Amish to hire their non-Amish neighbors to drive them.

*217. Railroad Crossing, dated 1928. Cotton, 86 x 61. Holmes Co., Ohio. The Darwin D. Bearley Collection. This variation uses a pinwheel patch in the center of each block surrounded by stacked triangles. A zigzag inner border adds to the drama of this quilt.*

*218. Railroad Crossing, c. 1920. Cotton, 75 x 79. Holmes Co., Ohio. Judi Boisson Antique American Quilts, New York. Unusually light colors are used throughout this quilt. Although the patches vary, their color schemes are obviously planned in a similar fashion.*

# Double Wedding Ring

The Double Wedding Ring is a design of great complexity and openness requiring much of its maker. Its light, airy feeling is achieved by interlocking pieced rings that surround circular fields that invite intricate quilting. The pattern must have been borrowed by Amish quiltmakers seeking a real challenge in piecing. The Double Wedding Ring pattern is difficult to execute because all sides of the patch are curved. This requires precision in both cutting and piecing so that the finished top will lay flat without gathers or puckers.

Quilting generally outlines the angled pieces within the rings plus creates an additional design inside each ring. Amish Double Wedding Ring quilts generally have borders that also contain generous quilting.

It is easy to understand the popularity of this design in general society. It is an appropriate choice for a wedding gift. However, in Amish circles, jewelry of all kinds, including wedding bands, is not permitted. So the Amish quiltmakers' fascination with this pattern must have been because of its complexity.

Although the Amish do not use wedding rings, they view marriage as a serious commitment, made for life. Divorce is almost unheard of among Amish groups. Marriages last because of the support system provided by a couple's families and church. They do not marry and rear children in isolation. They are nurtured and tended by a closeknit group of concerned friends who share a common faith-life.

Farmsteads often house three generations and although privacy is maintained by the third generation having separate quarters, grandparents, parents, and children have a great deal of interaction. One's closest neighbors are often family or other church members. Together they share in life's joys and sorrows.

*221. Double Wedding Ring, 1953. Cotton, 82 x 88. Arthur, Illinois. Rebecca Haarer. The white background and scalloped edge mark this as a later quilt. Although the date marks this quilt as later than most collected antique Amish quilts, it is included here as an example of a less conservative approach to color.*

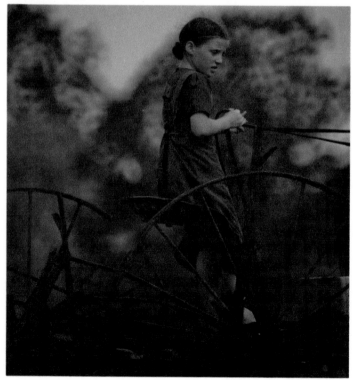

*Interlocking circular images are found in many places around the farm. Resembling the Double Wedding Ring pattern, the wheels of this implement serve important functions on Amish farmsteads.*

**223.** *Double Wedding Ring, dated 1952. Cotton, 73 x 93. Holmes Co., Ohio. Judi Boisson Antique American Quilts, New York. Bright colors stand out vividly against a black background. Pieced diamonds form a containing inner border. Spider web quilting designs fill the centers of the rings. Although a later quilt, it is done in colors typical of earlier Amish quilts in this pattern.*

**224,226.** *Reversible Double Wedding Ring, c. 1910. Cotton, 78 x 51. Ohio. Judi Boisson Antique American Quilts, New York. This unusual quilt has a pieced pattern on both sides. Note the quilted rings visible on the patchwork back below.*

**225.** *Double Wedding Ring-Diamond Border, 1920. Cotton, 72 x 82. Ohio. Judi Boisson Antique American Quilts, New York. These brightly colored rings are contained inside a pieced diamond border. The black background serves as a stark contrast to the colors of the small patches.*

# Diagonal Triangles

Triangles have always seemed to delight quilters. The angles and sharp points give a quilt vibrance and energy. Triangles appear in numerous complex patterns but are perfectly capable of standing alone. In the Diagonal Triangles pattern, light and dark triangles are pitted against each other forming jagged diagonal lines that shoot across the quilt top.

This quilt sparkles without fancy quilting. Its borders usually are filled with the typical Amish patterns of flowing quilting designs. The pieced body of the quilt generally has its triangles outlined in quilting stitches or simple straight lines are quilted across its top.

*227. Diagonal Triangles, 1929. Cotton, 76 x 70. Holmes Co., Ohio. Judi Boisson Antique American Quilts, New York. Several streaks of red give real zest to this dramatic quilt.*

*228. Diagonal Triangles, 1920-30. Cotton, 70 x 71. Holmes Co., Ohio. Judi Boisson Antique American Quilts, New York. An inner border of pieced diamonds outlines the sharp diagonal lines.*

# Drunkard's Path

Perhaps because the name has a negative connotation, perhaps because there are so many ways to organize it, this quilt has been called by an assortment of titles. Drunkard's Path is also known as Solomon's Puzzle, Old Maid Puzzle, Rocky Road to Kansas, Love Ring, None-Such, World Without End, and more.

No matter its name or arrangement it is a fascinating pattern. The blocks are a combination of positive and negative space. The section cut out of one patch creates a space to be filled by the adjoining patch. The result is a staggering path of patches across the quilt.

Piecing requires skill here because each patch has a curved edge. Care must be taken so that curves are smooth and flat. Assembly of the pieced blocks also demands clear thinking so that a consistent overall pattern is formed.

Quilting stitches generally follow the lines of the pieced design giving it an additional dimension. Empty space between patches and on borders provides additional space for quilting designs.

**229.** *Drunkard's Path, c. 1935-40. Cotton, 79 x 86. Collected LaGrange Co., probably made there. Rebecca Haarer. This is also a friendship quilt. Various patches were likely constructed by the persons whose names are embroidered on them. The patches were then collected and assembled by or for a common friend.*

**230.** *Drunkard's Path Variation, c. 1910. Cotton, 80 x 75. Ohio. Judi Boisson Antique American Quilts, New York. This assemblage of Drunkard's Path patches is also known as "World Without End," or "Ocean Waves."*

**231.** *Drunkard's Path, 1920-30. Cotton, 84 x 80. Withee, Wisconsin. Judi Boisson Antique American Quilts, New York. The addition of a sawtooth inner border brings angularity to an otherwise curved design.*

# Other Quilts

**232.** *Leaves, 1910. Cotton, 84 x 74. Loudenville, Ohio. Judi Boisson Antique American Quilts, New York. This quilt is unusual among Amish quilts both in pattern and technique. Most Amish quilts are pieced whereas this design is appliquéd.*

It is impossible to speak of the Amish in general and at the same time give an accurate portrayal of specific Amish groups. They are a living, vibrant people with great diversities.

The same is true of Amish quilts. One cannot categorize Amish quilts in a definitive way. There are always those exceptions, those one-of-a-kind quilts, the unnamed patterns, and unusual variations.

This final category is an attempt to show a few of those singular quilts. Some are not necessarily unusual, just less frequently found or collected. Others are one-of-a-kind quilts that show the real zest for life and vivid imagination that have inspired so many beautiful bedcovers.

Like the Amish themselves, these quilts cannot be labeled and shelved. They must be understood in their context. For these creative bedcovers—or works of art—become more startling when seen as a part of the very fabric of Amish life. Only then can they begin to tell their story.

**233.** *Pocket Scrapquilt (knotted comforter), c. 1930-40. Cotton, 84 x 73. Mifflin Co., Pennsylvania. The Darwin D. Bearley Collection. This quilt came from a community of Amish where pockets were not permitted on workshirts. These store-bought shirts were revised at home. The pockets form the pattern on this knotted comforter.*

**234.** *Original design: Scrapquilt, c. 1900-1925. Cotton, 93 x 78. Missouri or Kansas. Nancy Meng. This one-of-a-kind quilt exemplifies the spirit of imagination that has inspired so many beautiful Amish bedcovers.*

**235.** *Zig-zag, c. 1930. Cotton, 82 x 70. Elk-hart Co., Indiana. Joseph M. B. Sarah. A few snippets of printed fabric crept into the pieced border of this otherwise more typical quilt. It was made from scraps given by non-Amish friends.*

**236.** *Goose Tracks, dated 1871. Cotton, 79 x 64. Ohio. Judi Boisson Antique American Quilts, New York. Tiny diamonds and closely quilted straight lines add dimension to this sprightly pattern.*

**237.** *Crosses and Losses, c. 1900-10. Cotton, 64 x 82. Ohio. William B. Wigton. Strong borders contain the agitation created by brightly colored patches with sharp points.*

**238.** *Broken Dishes, c. 1925-30. Cotton, 71 x 62. Ohio. The Darwin D. Bearley Collection. This quilter apparently ran out of border fabric before the job was completed. She simply added a piece of black.*

**239.** *Rolling Stone, c. 1915. Cotton, wool, 59 x 72. Middlebury, Elkhart Co., Indiana. Mary Ann Ryman. Although all shapes are geometric the finished patch gives the illusion of rounded edges.*

**240.** *Wild Goose Variation, c. 1920-30. Cotton, 68 x 74. LaGrange Co., Indiana. Faye and Don Walters. Triangles in a multitude of colors create various shapes in combination with each other.*

**241.** *King's Cross Variation, c. 1930. Wool and cotton, 73 x 68. Kalona, Iowa. Kemp and Pat Beall. A simple design done in a myriad of colors creates a spectacular quilt.*

**242.** *Tree of Life, c. 1900. Wool, 81 x 65. Arthur, Illinois. Nancy Meng. Although showing signs of age, this quilt speaks to the exceptions in every rule. Few Amish women used this pattern as it would be considered a realistic representation of a tree.*

**243.** *New York Beauty, c. 1920-30. Cotton, 70 x 88. Ohio. Judi Boisson Antique American Quilts, New York. A very rare pattern among Amish quilts, this one must have been the work of an extremely adventuresome quilter. She must also have been quite skilled.*

**244.** *Bachelor's Puzzle, c. 1925. Cotton, 83 x 70. Collected Ohio. The Darwin D. Bearley Collection. This pattern is also known as Indiana Puzzle. The white zig-zag inner border adds to the turbulent feel of the quilt.*

125

# Song of a People

We watch the past create the now,
And wish to plant before we plow,
We hear goodbye in each hello,
And wish to stay when we must go,
We speak of peace in time of war,
And watch the rich receive the poor,
As day makes night a fugitive,
The living dream, the dreaming live.

*—Merle Good*

# Readings and Sources

## Cross Reference

Pellman, Rachel T. **Amish Quilt Patterns.** Good Books, Intercourse, Pennsylvania, 1984.

## About Antique Amish Quilts

Bishop, Robert and Elizabeth Safanda. **A Gallery of Amish Quilts.** E. P. Dutton and Company, Inc., New York, New York, 1976.

Haders, Phyllis. **Sunshine and Shadow: The Amish and Their Quilts.** Universe Books, New York, New York, 1976.

Horton, Roberta. **Amish Adventure.** C & T Publishing. Lafayette, California, 1983.

Lawson, Suzy. **Amish Inspirations.** Amity Publications. Cottage Grove, Oregon, 1982.

Pottinger, David. **Quilts from the Indiana Amish.** E. P. Dutton, Inc., New York, New York, 1983.

## About Other Quilts

Beyer, Jinny. **Patchwork Patterns.** EPM Publications, McLean, Virginia, 1979.

Danneman, Barbara. **Step by Step Quiltmaking.** Golden Press, Western Publishing Company, Inc., New York, New York, 1975.

Haders, Phyllis. **The Warner Collector's Guide to American Quilts.** The Main Street Press, New York, New York, 1981.

Hall, Carrie A. and Rose G. Kretsinger. **The Romance of the Patchwork Quilt in America.** Bonanza Books, New York, New York, 1935.

Hassel, Carla J. **You Can Be A Super Quilter!** Wallace-Homestead Book Company, Des Moines, Iowa, 1980.

Holstein, Jonathan. **The Pieced Quilt: An American Design Tradition.** New York Graphic Society, Boston, Massachusetts, 1973.

Houck, Carter and Myron Miller. **American Quilts and How To Make Them.** Charles Scribner's Sons, New York, New York, 1975.

Leone, Diana. **The Sampler Quilt.** Leone Publications, Santa Clara, California, 1980.

Murwin, Susan Aylsworth and Suzzy Chalfant Payne. **Quick and Easy Patchwork on the Sewing Machine.** Dover Publications, Inc., New York, New York, 1979.

Orlovsky, Patsy, and Myron Orlovsky. **Quilts in America.** McGraw Hill Book Company, New York, New York, 1974.

Pellman, Rachel T. and Joanne Ranck. **Quilts Among the Plain People.** Good Books, Intercourse, Pennsylvania. 1981.

## About the Amish

**Amish Cooking.** Pathway Publishers, Aylmer, Ontario, 1965.

Bender, H. S. **The Anabaptist Vision.** Herald Press, Scottdale, Pennsylvania, 1967.

Braght, Thieleman J. van, Comp. **The Bloody Theatre; or, Martyrs Mirror.** Scottdale, Pennsylvania, 1951.

**Budget, The.** Sugarcreek, Ohio, 1890. A weekly newspaper serving the Amish and Mennonite communities.

**Devoted Christian's Prayer Book.** Pathway Publishing House, Aylmer, Ontario, 1967.

**Family Life.** Amish periodical published monthly. Pathway Publishing House, Aylmer, Ontario.

Gingerich, Orland. **The Amish of Canada.** Conrad Press. Waterloo, Ontario, 1972.

Good, Merle and Phyllis Pellman Good. **20 Most Asked Questions about the Amish and Mennonites.** Good Books, Lancaster, Pennsylvania, 1979.

Good, Phyllis Pellman and Rachel Thomas Pellman. **From Amish and Mennonite Kitchens.** Good Books, Intercourse, Pennsylvania, 1984.

Hostetler, John A. **Amish Life.** Herald Press, Scottdale, Pennsylvania, 1959.

Hostetler, John A. **Amish Society.** Johns Hopkins University Press, Baltimore, Maryland, 1963.

Keim, Albert N. **Compulsory Education and the Amish.** Beacon Press, Boston, Massachusetts, 1975.

Klaassen, Walter. **Anabaptism: Neither Catholic nor Protestant.** Conrad Press, Waterloo, Ontario, 1972.

Schreiber, William I. **Our Amish Neighbors.** University of Chicago Press, Chicago, Illinois, 1962.

Schweider, Elmer and Dorothy Schweider. **A Peculiar People: Iowa's Old Order Amish.** Iowa State University Press, Ames, Iowa, 1975.

# Index

# About the Authors

Rachel Thomas Pellman is manager of The Old Country Store in Intercourse, Pennsylvania, which features quilts, crafts and toys made by more than 250 Amish and Mennonite craftspersons. A graduate of Eastern Mennonite College, she has written AMISH QUILT PATTERNS, a companion book to THE WORLD OF AMISH QUILTS. She has also co-authored QUILTS AMONG THE PLAIN PEOPLE, FROM AMISH AND MENNONITE KITCHENS, and 12 Pennsylvania Dutch Cookbooks.

Kenneth R. Pellman is manager of The People's Place, an educational center concerned with Amish and Mennonite arts, faith and culture. Kenny graduated from Eastern Mennonite College, where he taught drama for one year. His photography appears in several books, including a National Geographic publication. He is currently working on two more manuscripts that deal with Amish and Mennonite themes.

The Pellmans were married in 1976. They live in Lancaster, Pennsylvania with their young son, Nathaniel. They are members of the Rossmere Mennonite Church.